NYSTCE® Math

Practice Test Questions for the NYSTCE® Mathematics CST

Published by

Complete TEST Preparation Inc.

Copyright © 2016 by Complete Test Preparation Inc. ALL RIGHTS RESERVED.

No part of this book may be reproduced or transferred in any form or by any means, graphic, electronic, or mechanical, including photocopying, recording, web distribution, taping, or by any information storage retrieval system, without the written permission of the author.

Notice: Complete Test Preparation Inc. makes every reasonable effort to obtain from reliable sources accurate, complete, and timely information about the tests covered in this book. Nevertheless, changes can be made in the tests or the administration of the tests at any time and Complete Test Preparation Inc. makes no representation or warranty, either expressed or implied as to the accuracy, timeliness, or completeness of the information contained in this book. Complete Test Preparation Inc. make no representations or warranties of any kind, express or implied, about the completeness, accuracy, reliability, suitability or availability with respect to the information contained in this document for any purpose. Any reliance you place on such information is therefore strictly at your own risk.

The author(s) shall not be liable for any loss incurred as a consequence of the use and application, directly or indirectly, of any information presented in this work. Sold with the understanding, the author is not engaged in rendering professional services or advice. If advice or expert assistance is required, the services of a competent professional should be sought.

The company, product and service names used in this publication are for identification purposes only. All trademarks and registered trademarks are the property of their respective owners. Complete Test Preparation Inc. is not affiliated with any educational institution.

We strongly recommend that students check with exam providers for up-to-date information regarding test content.

NYSTCE®, New York State Teacher Certification Examinations, and the NYSTCE logo are trademarks of the New York State Education Department and Pearson Education, Inc. or its affiliate(s).

Published by
Complete Test Preparation Inc.
Victoria BC Canada

Visit us on the web at http://www.test-preparation.ca
Printed in the USA

ISBN-13: 9781772451689

Version 6.6 February 2017

About Complete Test Preparation

The Complete Test Preparation Team has been publishing high quality study materials since 2005. Thousands of students visit our websites every year, and thousands of students, teachers and parents all over the world have purchased our teaching materials, curriculum, study guides and practice tests.

Complete Test Preparation is committed to providing students with the best study materials and practice tests available on the market. Members of our team combine years of teaching experience, with experienced writers and editors, all with advanced degrees.

Feedback

We welcome your feedback. Email us at feedback@test-preparation.ca with your comments and suggestions. We carefully review all suggestions and often incorporate reader suggestions into upcoming versions. As a Print on Demand Publisher, we update our products frequently.

 **Find us on Facebook**

www.facebook.com/CompleteTestPreparation

The Environment and Sustainability

Environmental consciousness is important for the continued growth of our company. In addition to eco-balancing each title, as a print on demand publisher, we only print units as orders come in, which greatly reduces excess printing and waste. This revolutionary printing technology also eliminates carbon emissions from trucks hauling boxes of books everywhere to warehouses. We also maintain a commitment to recycling any waste materials that may result from the printing process. We continue to review our manufacturing practices on an ongoing basis to ensure we are doing our part to protect and improve the environment.

Contents

6   **Getting Started**
       The NYSTCE® Mathematics Study Plan   7

12   **Practice Test Questions Set 1 (Easy)**
       Skills and Competencies   46
       Answer Key   51

88   **Practice Test Questions Set 2 (More Difficult)**
       Skills and Competencies   124
       Answer Key   129

175   **Conclusion**

Getting Started

CONGRATULATIONS! By deciding to take the NYSTCE® Mathematics Test, you have taken the first step toward a great future! Of course, there is no point in taking this important examination unless you intend to do your best to earn the highest grade you possibly can. That means getting yourself organized and discovering the best approaches, methods and strategies to master the material. Yes, that will require real effort and dedication on your part, however, if you are willing to focus your energy and devote the study time necessary, before you know it you will be on you will be passing your exam with a great mark!

We know that taking on a new endeavour can be a little scary, and it is easy to feel unsure of where to begin. That's where we come in.

About the Exam

The NYSTCE® Mathematics 6 - 12 Test is composed of seven sections, Algebra, (Basic and Advanced) Functions, Calculus, Geometry, (including coordinate geometry) Trigonometry, Statistics and Probability, and Mathematical Reasoning.

While we seek to make our guide as comprehensive as possible, note that like all exams, the NYSTCE® Mathematics Test might be adjusted at some future point. New material might be added, or content that is no longer relevant or applicable might be removed. It is always a good idea to give the materials you receive when you register to take the test a careful review.

The NYSTCE® Mathematics Study Plan

Now that you have made the decision to take the NYSTCE® Mathematics, it is time to get started. Before you do another thing, you will need to figure out a plan of attack. The very best study tip is to start early! The longer the time period you devote to regular study practice, the more likely you will be to retain the material and be able to access it quickly. If you thought that 1x20 is the same as 2x10, guess what? It really is not, when it comes to study time. Reviewing material for just an hour per day over the course of 20 days is far better than studying for two hours a day for only 10 days. The more often you revisit a particular piece of information, the better you will know it. Not only will your grasp and understanding be better, but your ability to reach into your brain and quickly and efficiently pull out the tidbit you need, will be greatly enhanced as well.

The great Chinese scholar and philosopher Confucius believed that true knowledge could be defined as knowing both what you know and what you do not know. The first step in preparing for the NYSTCE Mathematics is to assess your strengths and weaknesses.

Making a Study Schedule

To make your study time most productive you will need to develop a study plan. The purpose of the plan is to organize all the bits of pieces of information in such a way that you will not feel overwhelmed. Rome was not built in a day, and learning everything you will need to know to pass the NYSTCE® Mathematics is going to take time, too. Arranging the material you need to learn into manageable chunks is the best way to go. Each study session should make you feel as though you have accomplished your goal, and your goal is simply to learn what you planned to learn during that particular session. Try to organize the content in such a way that each study session builds on previous ones. That way, you will retain the information, be better able to access it, and review the previous bits and pieces at the same time.

Self-assessment

The Best Study Tip! The very best study tip is to start early! The longer you study regularly, the more you will retain and 'learn' the material. Studying for 1 hour per day for 20 days is far better than studying for 2 hours for 10 days.

What don't you know?

The first step is to assess your strengths and weaknesses. You may already have an idea of where your weaknesses are, or you can take our Self-assessment modules for each of the areas, Reading Comprehension, Arithmetic, Essay Writing, Algebra and College Level Math.

Exam Component	Rate 1 to 5
Mathematical Reasoning	
Algebra	
Functions	
Calculus	
Geometry	
Statistics and Probability	

Making a Study Schedule

The key to making a study plan is to divide the material you need to learn into manageable size and learn it, while at the same time reviewing the material that you already know.

Using the table above, any scores of three or below, you need to spend time learning, going over and practicing this subject area. A score of four means you need to review the material, but you don't have to spend time re-learning. A score of five and you are OK with just an occasional review before the exam.

A score of zero or one means you really do need to work on this and you should allocate the most time and give it the highest priority. Some students prefer a 5-day plan and others a 10-day plan. It also depends on how much time you have until the exam.

Here is an example of a 5-day plan based on an example from the table above:

Mathematical Reasoning: 1   Study 1 hour everyday – review on last day
Algebra: 3   Study 1 hour for 2 days then ½ hour and then review
Functions: 4   Review every second day
Geometry: 2 Study 1 hour on the first day – then ½ hour everyday
Statistics and Probability: 5   Review for ½ hour every other day

Using this example, Geometry and Statistics and Probability are good, and only need occasional review. Functions are good and needs 'some' review. Algebra needs a bit of work and Mathematical Reasoning is very weak and needs the most time. Based on this, here is a sample study plan:

Day	Subject	Time
Monday		
Study	Mathematical Reasoning	1 hour
Study	Geometry	1 hour
	½ hour break	
Study	Algebra	1 hour
Review	Functions	½ hour
Tuesday		
Study	Mathematical Reasoning	1 hour
Study	Geometry	½ hour
	½ hour break	
Study	Algebra	½ hour
Review	Functions	½ hour
Wednes-day		
Study	Mathematical Reasoning	1 hour
Study	Geometry	½ hour
	½ hour break	
Study	Algebra	½ hour
Thursday		
Study	Mathematical Reasoning	½ hour
Study	Geometry	½ hour
Review	Algebra	½ hour
	½ hour break	
Review	Functions	½ hour
Friday		
Review	Mathematical Reasoning	½ hour
Review	Geometry	½ hour
Review	Algebra	½ hour
	½ hour break	
Review	Functions	½ hour
Review	Geometry	½ hour

Using this example, adapt the study plan to your own schedule. This schedule assumes 2 ½ - 3 hours available to study everyday for a 5 day period.

First, write out what you need to study and how much. Next figure out how many days you have before the test. Note, do NOT study on the last day before the test. On the last day before the test, you won't learn anything and will probably only confuse yourself.

Make a table with the days before the test and the number of hours you have available to study each day. We suggest working with 1 hour and ½ hour time slots.

Start filling in the blanks, with the subjects you need to study the most, getting the most time and the most regular time slots (i.e. everyday) and the subjects that you know getting the least time (e.g. ½ hour every other day, or every 3rd day).

Tips for Making a Schedule

Once you make a schedule, stick with it! Make your study sessions reasonable. If you make a study schedule and don't stick with it, you set yourself up for failure. Instead, schedule study sessions that are a bit shorter and set yourself up for success! Make sure your study sessions are do-able. Studying is hard work but after you pass, you can party and take a break!

Schedule breaks. Breaks are just as important as study time. Work out a rotation of studying and breaks that works for you.

Build up study time. If you find it hard to sit still and study for 1 hour straight-through, build up to it. Start with 20 minutes, and then take a break. Once you get used to 20-minute study sessions, increase the time to 30 minutes. Gradually work you way up to 1 hour.

40 minutes to 1 hour is optimal. Studying for longer than this is tiring and not productive. Studying for shorter isn't long enough to be productive.

Practice Test Questions Set 1 (Easy)

The questions below are not the same as you will find on the NYSTCE® Mathematics - that would be too easy! And nobody knows what the questions will be and they change all the time. Below are general questions that cover the same subject areas as the NYSTCE® Mathematics test. So, while the format and exact wording of the questions may differ slightly, and change from year to year, if you can answer the questions below, you will have no problem with the NYSTCE® Mathematics test.

In general, the questions in practice test set 1 are easier and the questions in practice set 2 are more difficult.

For the best results, take these practice test questions as if it were the real exam. Set aside time when you will not be disturbed, and a location that is quiet and free of distractions. Read the instructions carefully, read each question carefully, and answer to the best of your ability.
Use the bubble answer sheets provided. When you have completed the practice questions, check your answer against the Answer Key and read the explanation provided.

Do not attempt more than one set of practice test questions in one day. After completing the first practice test, wait two or three days before attempting the second set of questions.

Part I - Number and Quantity

1. Ⓐ Ⓑ Ⓒ Ⓓ   11. Ⓐ Ⓑ Ⓒ Ⓓ
2. Ⓐ Ⓑ Ⓒ Ⓓ   12. Ⓐ Ⓑ Ⓒ Ⓓ
3. Ⓐ Ⓑ Ⓒ Ⓓ   13. Ⓐ Ⓑ Ⓒ Ⓓ
4. Ⓐ Ⓑ Ⓒ Ⓓ   14. Ⓐ Ⓑ Ⓒ Ⓓ
5. Ⓐ Ⓑ Ⓒ Ⓓ   15. Ⓐ Ⓑ Ⓒ Ⓓ
6. Ⓐ Ⓑ Ⓒ Ⓓ   16. Ⓐ Ⓑ Ⓒ Ⓓ
7. Ⓐ Ⓑ Ⓒ Ⓓ   17. Ⓐ Ⓑ Ⓒ Ⓓ
8. Ⓐ Ⓑ Ⓒ Ⓓ   18. Ⓐ Ⓑ Ⓒ Ⓓ
9. Ⓐ Ⓑ Ⓒ Ⓓ   19. Ⓐ Ⓑ Ⓒ Ⓓ
10. Ⓐ Ⓑ Ⓒ Ⓓ   20. Ⓐ Ⓑ Ⓒ Ⓓ

Part II - Algebra

1. Ⓐ Ⓑ Ⓒ Ⓓ   11. Ⓐ Ⓑ Ⓒ Ⓓ
2. Ⓐ Ⓑ Ⓒ Ⓓ   12. Ⓐ Ⓑ Ⓒ Ⓓ
3. Ⓐ Ⓑ Ⓒ Ⓓ   13. Ⓐ Ⓑ Ⓒ Ⓓ
4. Ⓐ Ⓑ Ⓒ Ⓓ   14. Ⓐ Ⓑ Ⓒ Ⓓ
5. Ⓐ Ⓑ Ⓒ Ⓓ   15. Ⓐ Ⓑ Ⓒ Ⓓ
6. Ⓐ Ⓑ Ⓒ Ⓓ   16. Ⓐ Ⓑ Ⓒ Ⓓ
7. Ⓐ Ⓑ Ⓒ Ⓓ   17. Ⓐ Ⓑ Ⓒ Ⓓ
8. Ⓐ Ⓑ Ⓒ Ⓓ   18. Ⓐ Ⓑ Ⓒ Ⓓ
9. Ⓐ Ⓑ Ⓒ Ⓓ   19. Ⓐ Ⓑ Ⓒ Ⓓ
10. Ⓐ Ⓑ Ⓒ Ⓓ   20. Ⓐ Ⓑ Ⓒ Ⓓ

Part III - Functions

1. Ⓐ Ⓑ Ⓒ Ⓓ   11. Ⓐ Ⓑ Ⓒ Ⓓ
2. Ⓐ Ⓑ Ⓒ Ⓓ   12. Ⓐ Ⓑ Ⓒ Ⓓ
3. Ⓐ Ⓑ Ⓒ Ⓓ   13. Ⓐ Ⓑ Ⓒ Ⓓ
4. Ⓐ Ⓑ Ⓒ Ⓓ   14. Ⓐ Ⓑ Ⓒ Ⓓ
5. Ⓐ Ⓑ Ⓒ Ⓓ   15. Ⓐ Ⓑ Ⓒ Ⓓ
6. Ⓐ Ⓑ Ⓒ Ⓓ
7. Ⓐ Ⓑ Ⓒ Ⓓ
8. Ⓐ Ⓑ Ⓒ Ⓓ
9. Ⓐ Ⓑ Ⓒ Ⓓ
10. Ⓐ Ⓑ Ⓒ Ⓓ

Part IV - Calculus

1. Ⓐ Ⓑ Ⓒ Ⓓ
2. Ⓐ Ⓑ Ⓒ Ⓓ
3. Ⓐ Ⓑ Ⓒ Ⓓ
4. Ⓐ Ⓑ Ⓒ Ⓓ
5. Ⓐ Ⓑ Ⓒ Ⓓ
6. Ⓐ Ⓑ Ⓒ Ⓓ
7. Ⓐ Ⓑ Ⓒ Ⓓ
8. Ⓐ Ⓑ Ⓒ Ⓓ
9. Ⓐ Ⓑ Ⓒ Ⓓ
10. Ⓐ Ⓑ Ⓒ Ⓓ

Part V - Geometry and Measurement

1. Ⓐ Ⓑ Ⓒ Ⓓ   11. Ⓐ Ⓑ Ⓒ Ⓓ
2. Ⓐ Ⓑ Ⓒ Ⓓ   12. Ⓐ Ⓑ Ⓒ Ⓓ
3. Ⓐ Ⓑ Ⓒ Ⓓ   13. Ⓐ Ⓑ Ⓒ Ⓓ
4. Ⓐ Ⓑ Ⓒ Ⓓ   14. Ⓐ Ⓑ Ⓒ Ⓓ
5. Ⓐ Ⓑ Ⓒ Ⓓ   15. Ⓐ Ⓑ Ⓒ Ⓓ
6. Ⓐ Ⓑ Ⓒ Ⓓ
7. Ⓐ Ⓑ Ⓒ Ⓓ
8. Ⓐ Ⓑ Ⓒ Ⓓ
9. Ⓐ Ⓑ Ⓒ Ⓓ
10. Ⓐ Ⓑ Ⓒ Ⓓ

Part VI - Statistics and Probability

1. (A) (B) (C) (D)
2. (A) (B) (C) (D)
3. (A) (B) (C) (D)
4. (A) (B) (C) (D)
5. (A) (B) (C) (D)
6. (A) (B) (C) (D)
7. (A) (B) (C) (D)
8. (A) (B) (C) (D)
9. (A) (B) (C) (D)
10. (A) (B) (C) (D)

Part I - Number and Quantity

1. A car starts from a full stop and in 20 seconds is travelling 10/m per second. What is the acceleration?

    a. 0.5 m/sec²
    b. 0.24 m/sec²
    c. 1 m/sec²
    d. 1.5 m/sec²

2. Find the sum of the roots of the equation $\sqrt{[0.25^a]^{a-1}} = 2^{3a-3}$.

    a. -2
    b. -1
    c. 0
    d. 2

3. ((1 - 1/3) * (1 + 1/5)) / (1/8 * 4/5 - 1/3) =

    a. -24/7
    b. -7/24
    c. 7/24
    d. 24/7

4. $\sqrt{75} + \sqrt{48} - \sqrt{(3 / 0.01)} =$

    a. $-\sqrt{3}$
    b. $\sqrt{3}$
    c. 3
    d. $3\sqrt{3}$

5. x = a + bi and y = a - bi. If x * y = 5a², find one possible values of b in terms of a.

    a. a
    b. 2a
    c. 3a
    d. 4a

6. Find the determinant of matrix A = $\begin{bmatrix} 2 & -1 & 0 \\ 5 & 3 & 1 \\ 1 & 1 & -2 \end{bmatrix}$

    a. - 30
    b. - 25
    c. 10
    d. 15

7. Dylan has $2,000 in the bank paying an annual interest rate of 3.6%, compounded quarterly. After 9 years, how much money will Dylan have in the bank? Round your answer to the nearest integer.

    a. $2,543
    b. $2,761
    c. $4,634
    d. $6,647

8. Factor the polynomial $x^3y^3 - x^2y^8$.

    a. $x^2y^3(x - y^5)$
    b. $x^3y^3(1 - y^5)$
    c. $x^2y^2(x - y^6)$
    d. $xy^3(x - y^5)$

9. We are given that A = (√3 - 1) / (√5 + 1) and B = (√5 - 1) / (√3 + 1). What is the value of A in terms of B?

    a. B/2
    b. 3B/2
    c. 2B
    d. 3B

10.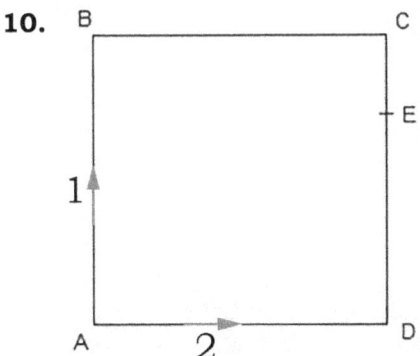

Two bicycles start moving from point A; one in direction 1, the other in direction 2. They first meet at point E. We know that 4|CE| = |CD| and ABCD is square. Find the ratio of the velocities V_1/V_2.

    a. 1/7
    b. 3/7
    c. 5/7
    d. 9/7

11. Write $1.3\overline{4}$ as a fraction.

    a. 41/90
    b. 43/90
    c. 23/30
    d. 121/90

12. Using the factoring method, solve the quadratic equation: $x^2 - 5x - 6 = 0$

    a. -6 and 1
    b. -1 and 6
    c. 1 and 6
    d. -6 and -1

13. Calculate $7 + 2 \times (6 + 3) \div 3 - 7$ using the order of operations

    a. 6
    b. 5
    c. 7
    d. 4

14. Sarah weighs 25 pounds more than Tony. If together they weigh 205 pounds, how much does Sarah weigh in kilograms? Assume 1 pound = 0.4535 kilograms.

    a. 41
    b. 48
    c. 50
    d. 52

15. A rocket releases a satellite into orbit around Earth. The satellite travels at 2000 m/second in 25 seconds. What is the acceleration?

    a. 0.2 m/sec^2
    b. -0.2 m/sec^2
    c. 5 m/sec^2
    d. 1 m/sec^2

16. A runner can sprint 6 meters per second. How far will she travel in 2 minutes?

    a. 720 meters

    b. 600 meters

    c. 500 meters

    d. 760 meters

17. 1000 N force is applied to a concrete block weighing 500 pounds. How fast will this force accelerate the block?

    a. 2 m/s^2

    b. 1 m/s^2

    c. 4 m/s^2

    d. 5 m/s^2

18. Find 2 numbers that sum to 21 and the sum of the squares is 261.

    a. 14 and 7

    b. 15 and 6

    c. 16 and 5

    d. 17 and 4

19. Using the factoring method, solve the quadratic equation: $x^2 + 4x + 4 = 0$

    a. 0 and 1

    b. 1 and 2

    c. 2

    d. -2

20. How fast can a person walk if they travel 1000 m in 20 minutes?

   a. 50 meters
   b. 75 meters
   c. 100 meters
   d. 125 meters

Part II - Algebra

1. $(3y^5 - 2y + y^4 + 2y^3 + 5) + (2y^5 + 3y^3 + 2 + 7y) =$

   a. $5y^5 + y^4 + 5y^3 + 5y + 7$
   b. $5y^3 + y^4 + 5y^3$
   c. $5y^5 + y^3 + 7y^3 + 5y + 5$
   d. $5y^2 + y^4 + 5y^3 + 7y + 5$

2. $(x^2 - 2)(3x^2 - 3x + 7) =$

   a. $3x^3 - 3x^3 + x^2 + 4x - 12$
   b. $3x^4 - 3x^3 + x^2 + 6x - 14$
   c. $3x^2 - 3x^3 + x + 6x - 10$
   d. $3x^2 - 3x + x + 4x - 14$

3. Solve the system: $4x - y = 5$; $x + 2y = 8$

   a. (3, 2)
   b. (3, 3)
   c. (2, 3)
   d. (2, 2)

4. Simplify the following expression:

$3x^3 + 2x^2 + 5x - 7 + 4x^2 - 5x + 2 - 3x^3$.

    a. $6x^2 - 9$
    b. $6x^2 - 5$
    c. $6x^2 - 10x - 5$
    d. $6x^2 + 10x - 9$

5.

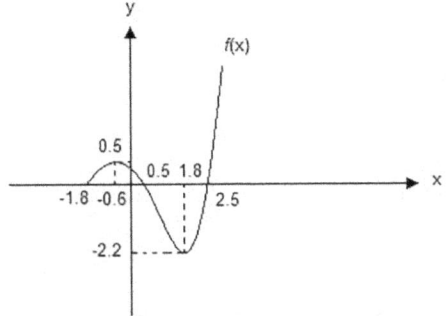

Using the graph of the function f, find
(f(1.8) - f(-1.8)) / f(-0.6).

    a. -4.4
    b. -3.8
    c. 2.8
    d. 4.0

6. Find the x-intercepts of the quadratic function
$f(x) = (x - 5)^2 - 9$.

    a. {2,4}
    b. {2,8}
    c. {4,8}
    d. {1,2}

7. Solve the inequality: $(2x + 1)/(2x - 1) < 1$.

   a. $(-2, +\infty)$
   b. $(1, +\infty)$
   c. $(-\infty, -2)$
   d. $(-\infty, 1/2)$

8. Using the quadratic formula, solve the following equation:

$(a^2 - b^2)x^2 + 2ax + 1 = 0$

   a. $a/(a + b)$ and $b/(a + b)$
   b. $1/(a + b)$ and $a/(a + b)$
   c. $a/(a + b)$ and $a/(a - b)$
   d. $-1/(a + b)$ and $-1/(a - b)$

9. Turn the following expression into a simple polynomial: $(a + b)(x + y) + (a - b)(x - y) - (ax + by)$

   a. $ax + by$
   b. $ax - by$
   c. $ax^2 + by^2$
   d. $ax^2 - by^2$

10. Given polynomials $A = 4x^5 - 2x^2 + 3x - 2$ and $B = -3x^4 - 5x^2 - 4x + 5$, find $A + B$.

   a. $x^5 - 3x^2 - x - 3$
   b. $4x^5 - 3x^4 + 7x^2 + x + 3$
   c. $4x^5 - 3x^4 - 7x^2 - x + 3$
   d. $4x^5 - 3x^4 - 7x^2 - x - 7$

11. Find 2 numbers whose difference is 11 and product is -24. (There is more than one solution.)

    a. (3,-8)

    b. (-3,8)

    c. (-3,-8)

    d. (3,8)

12. Find the sides of a right triangle whose sides are consecutive numbers.

    a. 1, 2, 3

    b. 2, 3, 4

    c. 3, 4, 5

    d. 4, 5, 6

13. Solve the linear equation: $-x - 7 = -3x - 9$

    a. -1

    b. 0

    c. 1

    d. 2

14. Solve the linear equation:
$3(x + 2) - 2(1 - x) = 4x + 5$

    a. -1

    b. 0

    c. 1

    d. 2

15. Line d_1 is parallel to line d_2, and the equation of line d_2 is $y = 3x + 2$. Which of the following cannot be the equation of line d_1?

    a. $3y = 9x - 8$
    b. $y = -2x + 2$
    c. $y = 3x + 5$
    d. $-4y = 5 - 12x$

16. The rate of my age to my brother's is 2/5 and the rate of my brother's age to our cousin's is 3/7. Find the rate of my age to my cousin's.

    a. 6/35
    b. 1/5
    c. 1/4
    d. 7/24

17. Simplify the expression $((8x^3 - 1) / (12x^2 + 6x + 3)) : ((2x - 1) / (x + 1))$.

    a. $(x^2 - 3) / (2x - 1)$
    b. $(x - 1) / 3$
    c. $(x + 1) / 3$
    d. $(8x^2 + 1) / (x + 1)$

18. In a store, the price of t-shirts and pants are constant. If John buys 4 t-shirts and 5 pair of pants, he pays $51. If he buys 7 t-shirts and 3 pair of pants, then he pays $49. Find the difference between the price of one pair of pants and one t-shirt.

    a. 0
    b. 3
    c. 7
    d. 12

19. Which of the following graphs represent the equation 4x - y = 6?

a.
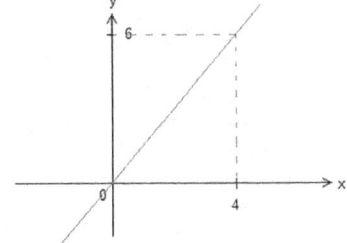

b.
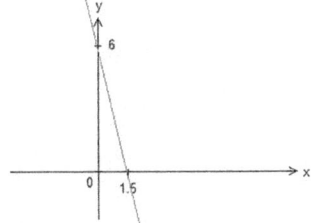

c.
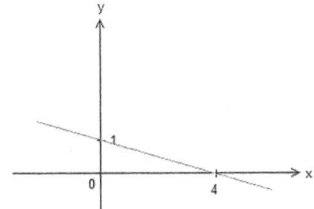

d.
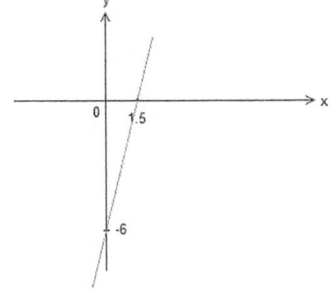

20. Find the answer choice which does not determine a function.

a. f = {(0, 2), (1, 5), (5, 5), (3, 0)}
b. y = 4x²

c.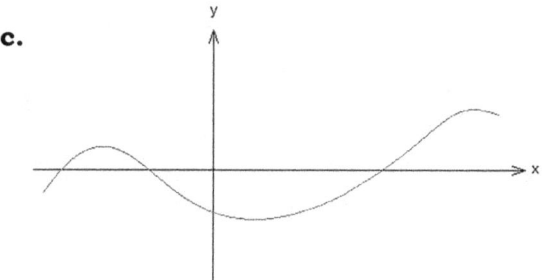

d.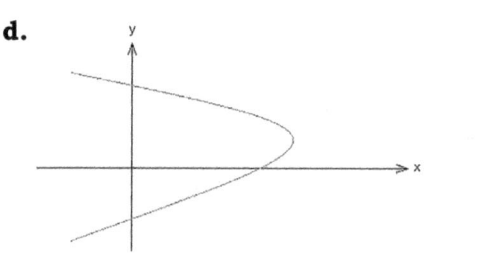

Part III - Functions

1. Describe the end behavior for the function f(x) = -2x⁵ + 3x + 97.

    a. Up on the left and right.
    b. Down on the left and right.
    c. Down on the left, up on the right.
    d. Up on the left, down on the right.

2. Given $g(x) = x^2 - 2$ and $h(x) = (x^2 - 2)^3$, find the first derivative of the function $f(x) = g(x) * h(x)$.

   a. $4(x^2 - 2)^3$
   b. $8x(x^2 - 2)^3$
   c. $4x^2 - 8$
   d. $(x^2 - 2)^3$

3. Find the antiderivative of $1/x + x^3 - \cos x$.

   a. $\ln x + x^4/4 + \sin x + C$
   b. $\ln x + x^4 - \sin x + C$
   c. $\ln x + x^4/4 - \sin x + C$
   d. $x^2 + x^4/4 - \sin x + C$

4. The general term of the sequence $\{a_n\}$ is 7^{2n-5}. How many times a_n is equal to a_{n+2}?

   a. 7^{-1}
   b. 7
   c. 7^2
   d. 7^4

5. A function is defined as $f(x) = \begin{cases} x > 1; \ x^3 + 2 \\ x \leq 1; \ -x/2 \end{cases}$

What is $(f(1) * f(3) - f(0)) / f^2(2)$ equal to?

   a. 0.130
   b. -0.145
   c. 0.200
   d. -0.240

6. If f(x) = -x, g(x) = 2x + 1 and h(x) = x^2, find f∘g∘h .

   a. x^2 - 1
   b. -$2x^2$ - 1
   c. x^2 - 2
   d. x^2 + 1

7. Find the inverse function of the function f(x) = 3x + 3.

   a. (3x - 1)/3
   b. (x + 1)/3
   c. (x - 1)/3
   d. (x - 3)/3

8. Find the inverse function of the function f(x) = (5x - 2)/4.

   a. (4x - 1)/5
   b. (x + 4)/5
   c. (4x + 2)/5
   d. (4x - 2)/5

9. Find f^{-1}(1/2) if f(x) = 1 - x.

   a. 1
   b. 1/2
   c. 1/3
   d. 1/4

10. Find the sum of the first 10 terms of the sequence 3, 6, 12, ...

   a. 189
   b. 765
   c. 3069
   d. 6141

11. Find the solution of equation $\log_2(3x + 11) - \log_2(x + 2) = 2$.

a. 2

b. 3

c. 5

d. 6

12. The revenue of a company on day t during March 2015 can be represented by the trigonometric function $M(t) = 50{,}000 - 350 \sin(2\pi t / 31)$ in dollars. What is the maximum revenue for the company this month?

a. $350

b. $49,650

c. $50,000

d. $50,350

13. Determine the domain and the range of the table below:

x	y
-5	18
4	15
2	9
7	4
12	-3

a. domain: {-3, 4, 9, 15, 18} range: {-5, 4, 2, 7, 12}

b. domain: {9, 11, 11, 13, 19} range: {-3, 4, 9, 15, 18}

c. domain: {-5, 2, 4, 7, 12} range: {-3, 4, 9, 15, 18}

d. domain: {9, 11, 13, 19} range: {-3, 4, 9, 15, 18}

14. Find the domain of the function √(x - 5) / (x + 5).

    a. (-∞, 5]
    b. (- 5, -∞)
    c. [5, +∞)
    d. [-∞, +∞)

15.

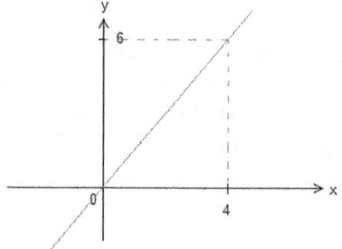

Above is the graph of a vehicle moving on a road. The distance travelled is given by time. Find the rate of change in m/s.

    a. 1.25 m/s
    b. 2.50 m/s
    c. 5.00 m/s
    d. 6.75 m/s

Part IV - Calculus

1. Calculate the definite integral $\int 2x^{-3}dx$.

    a. -5/36
    b. -5/72
    c. 1/18
    d. 2

2. Given $G(x) = \int_{x}^{\pi/4} \cos^2 3x \, dx$, find $G'(\pi/6)$.

   a. 0
   b. 1
   c. 1/2
   d. √3 / 2

3. Given that $\int_{-1}^{3} f(x)dx = -15$ and $\int_{3}^{-1} g(x)dx = 8$, find the value of $\int_{-1}^{3}(4g(x) - 5f(x))dx$.

   a. -107
   b. -43
   c. 43
   d. 107

4. Which of the following statements is correct?

   a. If the first derivative of the function is positive, then the function is decreasing.

   b. If the first derivative of the function is negative, then the function is increasing.

   c. If the second derivative of the function is positive, then the function is concave down.

   d. If the second derivative of the function is negative, then the function is concave down.

5. Using the first 5 terms of the Taylor Series 1 / (1 - x), find the approximate value of 5/4. Round your answer to the nearest hundredths.

    a. 1.20
    b. 1.23
    c. 1.24
    d. 1.25

6. A cylindrical tank is filled with water with a rate of 8cm³/min. Find the rate at which the height of the water is increasing. The radius of the tank is 2 cm.

    a. $2/\pi$
    b. 3
    c. π
    d. 2π

7. Using the method of separation of variables, find y in terms of x in $dy/dx = x^3/y^2$.

    a. $y = x^{3/2} + C$
    b. $y = \sqrt{(x^{2/3} + C)}$
    c. $y = \sqrt[3]{(3x^4/4 + 3C)}$
    d. $y = \sqrt[4]{(x^3/4 - 3C)}$

8. Using the limit definition, compute the derivative of $f(x) = 3x^2 - 2x + 7$.

    a. $6x^2 + 7$
    b. $6x - 2$
    c. $-2x + 7$
    d. $x^3 + 7x$

9. Given $F(x) = \int_{4}^{x} x^5 dx$, find $F'(3)$.

    a. 243
    b. 475
    c. 576
    d. 810

10. Find the local minimum of the function $6x^3 - 36x + 23$.

    a. (-2, -36)
    b. (2, 36)
    c. $(-\sqrt{2}, -36\sqrt{2})$
    d. $(\sqrt{2}, 36\sqrt{2})$

Part V - Geometry and Measurement

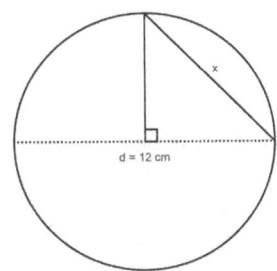

Note: Figure not drawn to scale

1. Calculate the length of side x.

    a. 6.46
    b. 8.48
    c. 3.6
    d. 6.4

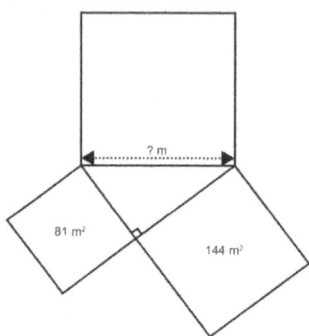

Note: figure not drawn to scale

2. What is the length of each side of the indicated square above? Assume the 3 shapes around the center triangle are square.

    a. 10
    b. 15
    c. 20
    d. 5

3. Reflect the parallelogram ABCD with the given mirror line m.

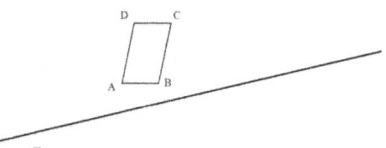

4. Reflect the circle with the center in O with the given mirror line m.

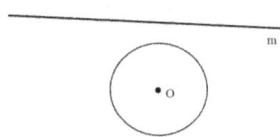

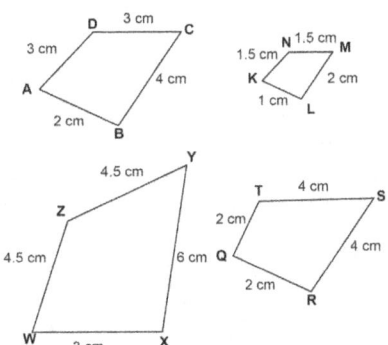

5. Which of the above quadrilaterals are similar?

    a. All are similar

    b. QRST, KLMN, WXYZ

    c. ABCD, KLMN, WXYZ

    d. All are different

6. In a class, there are 8 students who take only dancing lessons. 5 students take both dancing and singing lessons. The number of students taking singing lessons is 1 less than 2 times the number of students taking dancing lessons only. If 4 students take neither of these courses, how many students are in the class?

    a. 19
    b. 25
    c. 27
    d. 42

7. The interior angles of a triangle are given as $2x + 5$, $6x$ and $3x - 23$. Find the supplementary of the largest angle.

    a. $64°$
    b. $72°$
    c. $100°$
    d. $108°$

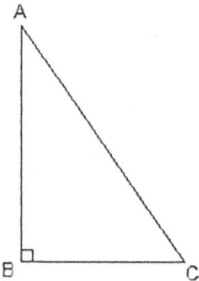

8. In the right triangle above, $|AB| = 2|BC|$ and $|AC| = 15$ cm. Find the length of $|AB|$.

    a. 5 cm
    b. 10 cm
    c. $5\sqrt{5}$ cm
    d. $6\sqrt{5}$ cm

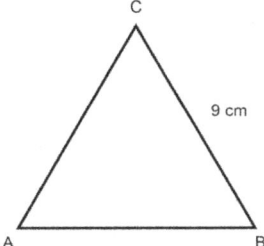

Note: figure not drawn to scale

9. What is the perimeter of the equilateral △ABC above?

    a. 18 cm
    b. 12 cm
    c. 27 cm
    d. 15 cm

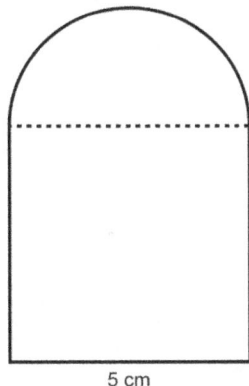

Note: figure not drawn to scale

10. What is the perimeter of the above shape, assuming the bottom portion is square?

    a. 22.85 cm
    b. 20 π cm
    c. 15 π cm
    d. 25 π cm

11. Find the range of the graph of
$x^2 + y^2 - 2x + 6y + 10 = 0$.

    a. [-1, 1]

    b. -3

    c. [-3, 3]

    d. {1, 3}

12. The line ay = 3x + 5 is parallel to the line 6y - x - 7 = 0. What is the value of a?

    a. 6

    b. 11

    c. 15

    d. 18

13. Find the area of the shape below:

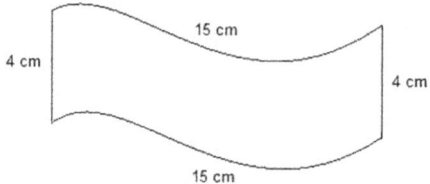

Note: figure not drawn to scale

    a. 19 cm²

    b. 45 cm²

    c. 60 cm²

    d. 90 cm²

14. What year was Euclidian geometry disproven, and by whom?

    a. Thales - BC 500s

    b. Pythagor BC 500s

    c. Pierre De Fermat 1600s

    d. Nikolai Lobachevsky 1830s

15. Which postulate below disproves Euclidean geometry?

 a. Through any two points, there is exactly one line.

 b. If equals are added to equals, the wholes are equal.

 c. Parallel postulate

 d. Things which coincide with one another are equal to one another (Reflexive property).

Part VI - Statistics and Probability

1. There are 3 blue, 1 white and 4 red identical balls inside a bag. If it is aimed to take two balls out of the bag consecutively, what is the probability to have 1 blue and 1 white ball?

 a. 3/28

 b. 1/12

 c. 1/7

 d. 3/7

2. Find the mean of these set of numbers: 100, 1050, 320, 600 and 150

 a. 333

 b. 444

 c. 440

 d. 320

3. Claire is playing a dart game and throwing the dart for 6 times. The probability to hit the board is 1/6. What is the probability to strike 4 times?

 a. 0.008

 b. 0.08

 c. 0.8

 d. 0.2

4. A boy has 4 red, 5 green and 2 yellow balls. He chooses two balls randomly for play. What is the probability that one is red and other is green?

   a. 2/11
   b. 19/22
   c. 20/121
   d. 9/11

5. A company, surveys a random sample of 120 employees about the number of days next month they prefer to eat out, instead of at the company cafeteria. 80 expected to eat out 5 days next month. There are 450 employees in the company. Based on the data, find the most reasonable estimate for the number of employees who expect to eat out 5 days next month.

   a. 240
   b. 300
   c. 360
   d. 390

6. Find the median of the set of numbers – 1,2,3,4,5,6,7,8,9 and 10

   a. 55
   b. 10
   c. 1
   d. 5.5

7. The following represents age distribution of students in an elementary class. Find the mode of the values – 7, 9, 10, 13, 11, 7, 9, 19, 12, 11, 9, 7, 9, 10, 11

   a. 7
   b. 9
   c. 10
   d. 11

8. There are 5 blue, 5 green and 5 red books on a shelf. Two books are selected randomly. What is the probability of choosing two books of different colors?

   a. 1/3
   b. 2/5
   c. 4/7
   d. 5/7

9. How many different ways can a reader choose 3 books out of 4, ignoring the order of selection?

   a. 3
   b. 4
   c. 9
   d. 12

10.

x	0	1	2	3	4	5
P(x = x_i)	0.30	0.25	0.20	0.12	0.10	0.03

In the table above, x is the number of cars that a salesperson sells per day. Having the related coincidence variables, what is the expected value?

   a. 1.03
   b. 1.40
   c. 1.56
   d. 2.33

Skills and Competencies

Number and Quantity

1. Solve acceleration problems

2. Perform operations with radical and rational numbers

3. Perform operations with rational numbers

4. Perform operations with radical and rational numbers

5. Perform operations with complex numbers

6. Operations on matrices

7. Solve compound interest word problems

8. Perform operations with Quadratics

9. Solve equations with rational or radical expressions

10. Solve problems involving velocity and quantities using vectors

11. Infinite decimal expansion

12. Perform operations with quadratics

13. Solve problems with order of operation

14. Solve word problems

15. Solve acceleration problems

16. Solve speed (Velocity) problems

17. Solve problems involving force

18. Solve problems with quadratics

19. Perform operations with quadratics

20. Solve speed (Velocity) problems

Algebra

1. Perform operations with polynomials

2. Perform operations with polynomials

3. Solve systems of linear equations in 2 variables

4. Simplify quadratic equations

5. Graphs of functions

6. Find intercepts of graphs of quadratics

7. Solve inequalities

8. Solve quadratic equations using different methods

9. Perform operations with polynomials

10. Perform operations with polynomials

11. Solve Solve real world problems with quadratics

12. Solve Solve real world problems with quadratics

13. Solve systems of linear equations in 1 variable

14. Solve systems of linear equations in 1 variable

15. Identify the equation of a line that is perpendicular or parallel to a given line

16. Analyze rates and proportional relationships and use them to solve real-world mathematical problems

17. Rewrite and manipulate rational expressions

18. Create equations and inequalities in two variables to describe relationships

19. Represent equations graphically

20. Evaluate whether a particular mathematical model (e.g., graph) describes a given set of conditions

Functions

1. Describe the behavior of functions

2. Calculate the first derivative of a function

3. Calculate antiderivatives

4. Solve questions involving arithmetic sequences

5. Perform operations with functions

6. Perform operations with functions

7. Calculate the inverse of functions

8. Calculate the inverse of functions

9. Perform operations with functions

10. Calculate arithmetic and geometric sequences

11. Solve problems involving logarithmic and exponential functions

12. Model periodic phenomena with trigonometric functions

13. Determine the domain and range of a given table of values

14. Calculate the domain of a function

15. Calculate rates of change

Calculus

1. Calculate definite integrals

2. Calculate the first derivative of a function

3. Interpret derivatives and definite integrals as limits (difference quotients)

4. Understand first derivatives of a function

5. Calculate power series

6. Use derivatives - to solve rates of change

7. Use first order differential equations to solve separation of variables and initial value problems.

8. Calculate the derivative of a function as a limit

9. Use the fundamental theorem of calculus to solve problems

10. Find local minimum and maximums of functions

Part V - Geometry and Measurement

1. Solve problems with Apply the Pythagorean theorem to solve problems

2. Solve problems with Apply the Pythagorean theorem to solve problems

3. Determine the reflected images of geometric objects on a coordinate plane

4. Determine the reflected images of geometric objects on a coordinate plane

5. Determine similarity of geometric objects

6. Solve problems with open and closed sets

7. Solve problems with lines, angles, triangles, parallelograms

8. Use trigonometry to solve problems with right triangles

9. Calculate perimeter

10. Calculate perimeter

11. Translate descriptions & equations of conic sections

12. Solve problems involving parallel lines

13. Calculate area and volume using Cavalieri's principle

14. Non-Euclidean geometry

15. Euclidean geometry

Part VI - Statistics and Probability

1. Calculate probability with dependent values

2. Calculate the mean of a set of data

3. Understand binomial distribution and probability distribution

4. Calculate simple probability

5. Make inferences about a population from a single random sample

6. Calculate median

7. Calculate mode

8. Calculate independence and conditional probability

9. Use probability/permutations and combinations to compute probabilities of compound events

10. Calculate expected value

Answer Key

Part I - Number and Quantity

1. A
The formula for acceleration = $A = (V_f - V_0)/t$

so $A = (10 \text{ m/sec} - 0 \text{ m/sec})/20 \text{ sec} = 0.5 \text{ m/sec}^2$

2. A
The roots of the equation are the possible values of a. To obtain the values of a; first, take the square of both sides:

$\sqrt{[0.25^a]^{a-1}} = 2^{3a-3}$

$(\sqrt{[0.25^a]^{a-1}})^2 = (2^{3a-3})^2$

$[0.25^a]^{a-1} = 2^{6a-6}$

Now, multiply the powers of 0.25 on the left hand side and remember that $0.25 = 1/4$ that is equal to 2^{-2}:

$2^{-2a^2 + 2a} = 2^{6a-6}$ ... Since both sides are on base 2, the powers should be equal:

$-2a^2 + 2a = 6a - 6$

$-2a^2 - 4a + 6 = 0$ ... Simplifying each term by -2:

$a^2 + 2a - 3 = 0$ ... Factorizing the quadratic function:

$(a + 3)(a - 1) = 0$

$a + 3 = 0$ OR $a - 1 = 0$

$a = -3$ OR $a = 1$ satisfy the equation. So, the sum of the roots of the equation is $-3 + 1 = -2$.

3. A
$((1 - 1/3) * (1 + 1/5)) / (1/8 * 4/5 - 1/3)$
First, do the operations inside parenthesis and the multiplication. In the numerator, we need to do one subtraction and one addition operation:

= ((3/3 - 1/3) * (5/5 + 1/5)) / (4 / (8 * 5) - 1/3)

Now, we can subtract and add the fractions having the same denominators. Also, in the denominator; numbers 4 and 8 can be simplified by 4:

= (2/3 * 6/5) / (1/10 - 1/3)

Here, 3 and 6 are simplified by 3; meanwhile, the subtraction operation in the denominator is performed using the LCM, (least common multiplier) which is 30 for 3 and 10:

= (4/5) / (3/30 - 10/30)

= (4/5) / ((3 - 10) / 30)

= (4/5) / (-7/30)

Now, we have two fractions that are divided. We can turn this operation into multiplication by simply changing the values of the denominator and the numerator of the second fraction as below:

= (4/5) * (- 30/7)

Note that we use parenthesis since the second fraction is negative. We can also write the minus sign in the front of the expression. Now, we can simplify 30 and 5 by 5:
= -4 * 6 / 7 = -24/7

4. A
Here, we see that the numbers inside the roots are not prime numbers, so we may find perfect square multipliers inside these numbers. Then, we can take these numbers out of the root as factors:

$\sqrt{75} + \sqrt{48} - \sqrt{3 / 0.01} = \sqrt{(3.25)} + \sqrt{(3.16)} - \sqrt{(3 / 0.01)}$

$= \sqrt{(3.5^2)} + \sqrt{(3.4^2)} - \sqrt{(3 / 0.1^2)}$

$= 5\sqrt{3} + 4\sqrt{3} - (1/0.1)\sqrt{3}$

Here, notice that 1/0.1 = 10/1 = 10:

$= (5 + 4 - 10)\sqrt{3}$

$= -\sqrt{3}$

5. B

In this type of questions, it is essential to recall that $i^2 = -1$.

We are given that x = a + bi and y = a - bi. To find x * y, we need to multiply these two expressions:

$x * y = (a + bi)(a - bi) = a^2 - abi + abi - b^2i^2 = a^2 + b^2$
So, $x * y = a^2 + b^2 = 5a^2$

Then, $b^2 = 4a^2$

To obtain b alone, let us take the square root of both sides:
$\sqrt{b^2} = \sqrt{(4a^2)}$

b = 2a and b = -2a

There are two possible solutions for b: 2a and -2a. We only find 2a in the answer choices.

6. B

The determinant of a matrix is found by the formula:
$\det A = a_{11} \det A_{11} - a_{12} \det A_{12} + a_{13} \det A_{13} - \ldots + (-1)^{1+n} a_{1n} \det A_{1n}$

$= \sum_{j=1}^{n} (-1)^{1+j} a_{1j} \det A_{1j}$

Here, A_{1j} named matrices are the submatrices obtained by closing 1st row and column j in the matrix A. The closed row and column elements are eliminated and the remaining entries form A_{1j} submatrices. The determinant of a 2 x 2 matrix is obtained by:

If $A = \begin{bmatrix} a & b \\ c & d \end{bmatrix}$, $\det A = ab - cd$.

So, in this question:

$\det A = \begin{bmatrix} 2 & -1 & 0 \\ 5 & 3 & 1 \\ 1 & 1 & -2 \end{bmatrix}$

$$= 2\begin{bmatrix} 3 & 1 \\ 1 & -2 \end{bmatrix} - (-1)\begin{bmatrix} 5 & 1 \\ 1 & -2 \end{bmatrix} + 0\begin{bmatrix} 5 & 3 \\ 1 & 1 \end{bmatrix}$$

= 2 (3(-2) - 1*1) + 1(5(-2) - 1 * 1) + 0(5 * 1 - 3 * 1)
= 2(-7) + (-11) + 0
= -14 - 11
= -25

7. B
The compound interest formula is as follows:
A = P * (1 + r/n) n * t

where,

P: initial amount deposited in the bank
r: annual rate of interest (written in decimal form)
n: number of times the interest is compounded per year
t: number of years passing
A: amount of money accumulated in the bank, including the interest

Inserting the values given in the question:

A = 2,000 (1 + 0.036/4) 4.9
= 2,000 (1.009)36
≈ 2,000 (1.380645)
= 2,761.29

When rounded to the nearest integer; Dylan will have approximately $2,761 in the bank.

8. A
We need to find the greatest common divisor of the two terms to factor the expression. We should remember that if the bases of exponent numbers are the same, the multiplication of two terms is found by summing the powers on the same base. Similarly; when dividing, the power of the divisor is subtracted from the power of the divided.

Both x^3y^3 and x^2y^8 contain x^2 and y^3. So,

$x^3y^3 - x^2y^8 = x * x^2y^3 - y^5 * x^2y^3$ ... We can carry x^2y^3 out as the factor:

$= x^2y^3(x - y^5)$

9. A
Notice the denominator of A and numerator of B; numerator of A and denominator of B are conjugates. If we equate the denominators of both A and B with the same number; it is easier to write A in terms of B.

$A = (\sqrt{3} - 1) / (\sqrt{5} + 1)_{(\sqrt{3} + 1)}$

$= ((\sqrt{3} - 1) * (\sqrt{3} + 1)) / ((\sqrt{5} + 1) * (\sqrt{3} + 1)) = (3 - 1) / ((\sqrt{5} + 1) * (\sqrt{3} + 1))$
$= 2 / ((\sqrt{5} + 1) * (\sqrt{3} + 1))$

$B = (\sqrt{5} - 1) / (\sqrt{3} + 1)_{(\sqrt{5} + 1)}$

$= ((\sqrt{5} - 1) * (\sqrt{5} + 1)) / ((\sqrt{5} + 1) * (\sqrt{3} + 1))$

$= (5 - 1) / ((\sqrt{5} + 1) (\sqrt{3} + 1))$

$= 4 / ((\sqrt{5} + 1) * (\sqrt{3} + 1))$

There is no need to expand the denominators of the new forms of A and B since they are the same. Comparing the numerators is sufficient. Notice that B is 2 times A. So A = B/2.

10. D
Bicycle 1 follows the path passing through points A - B - C - E; bicycle 2 follows A - D - E. We are given that 4|CE| = |CD| and the whole path is square shaped. Let us say that the length of one side is 4a. Then;

    1. Bicycle 1 goes 4a + 4a + a = 9a

    2. Bicycle 2 goes 4a + 3a = 7a distance. Since they meet at E; the ratio of their velocities is equal to the ratio of distances they have taken:

    3. $V_1/V_2 = 9a/7a = 9/7$

11. D
Say that x = 1.34444...

Our aim is to eliminate the repeating part (that is 4444...) to write x as a fraction. We need to write the appropriate 10th factors of x and do subtraction operation:

$100x = 134.4444...$
$- 10x = 13.4444...$
$90x = 121$

x = 121/90

12. B
$x^2 - 5x - 6 = 0$

We try to separate the middle term -5x to find common factors with x^2 and -6 separately:

$x^2 - 6x + x - 6 = 0$ ... Here, we see that x is a common factor for x^2 and -6x:

$x(x - 6) + x - 6 = 0$ ... Here, we have x times x - 6 and 1 time x - 6 summed up. This means that we have x + 1 times x - 6:

$(x + 1)(x - 6) = 0$ ... This is true when, either, or both the expressions in the parenthesis are equal to zero:

x + 1 = 0 ... x = -1

x - 6 = 0 ... x = 6

-1 and 6 are the solutions for this quadratic equation.

13. A
$7 + 2 \times (6 + 3) \div 3 - 7 = 6$

14. D
Let us denote Sarah's weight by "x." Then, since she weighs 25 pounds more than Tony, he will be x - 25. Together they weigh 205 pounds which means that the sum of the two representations will be equal to 205:
Sarah : x

Tony : x - 25

x + (x - 25) = 205 ... by arranging this equation we have:

x + x - 25 = 205

2x - 25 = 205 ... we add 25 to each side to have the x term alone:

2x - 25 + 25 = 205 + 25

2x = 230

x = 230/2

x = 115 pounds → Sarah weighs 115 pounds. Since 1 pound is 0.4535 kilograms, we need to multiply 115 by 0.4535 to have her weight in kilograms:

x = 115 * 0.4535 = 52.1525 kilograms → this is equal to 52 when rounded to the nearest whole number.

15. B
The formula for acceleration = $A = (V_f - V_0)/t$

so $A = (0 - 12)/60$ sec = -0.2 m/sec^2

16. A
Speed = (distance)/(time)
6 = x/120   (convert minutes to seconds)
6 * 120 = x
x = 720 meters

17. A
Force = Mass times Acceleration Measured in Newtons.
1000 = 500 x A
A = 1000/500 = 2 m/s^2

18. B
There are two statements made, which can be written as two equations:

The sum of two numbers are 21: x + y = 21

The sum of the squares is 261: $x^2 + y^2 = 261$

We are asked to find x and y.

Since we have the sums of the numbers and the sums of

their squares; we can use the square formula of x + y, that is:

$(x + y)^2 = x^2 + 2xy + y^2$ ... Here, we can insert the known values x + y and $x^2 + y^2$:

$(21)^2 = 261 + 2xy$ ... Arranging to find xy:

441 = 261 + 2xy

441 - 261 = 2xy

180 = 2xy

xy = 180/2

xy = 90

We need to find two numbers which multiply to 90. Checking the answer choices, we see that in (b), 15 and 6 are given, which sum to 90 (15 * 6 = 90) and their squares sum to 261 ($15^2 + 6^2$ = 225 + 36 = 261).

19. D
$x^2 + 4x + 4 = 0$ ... We try to separate the middle term 4x to find common factors with x^2 and 4 separately:

$x^2 + 2x + 2x + 4 = 0$ ... Here, we see that x is a common factor for x^2 and 2x, and 2 is a common factor for 2x and 4:

x(x + 2) + 2(x + 2) = 0 ... Here, we have x times x + 2 and 2 times x + 2 summed up. This means that we have x + 2 times x + 2:

(x + 2)(x + 2) = 0

$(x + 2)^2 = 0$ ... This is true if only if x + 2 is equal to zero.

x + 2 = 0

x = -2

20. A
Speed = (total distance traveled)/(total time taken)

X = 1000m/20 minutes

X = 50 meters

Part II - Algebra

1. A
Write in standard form $(3y^5 + y^4 + 2y^3 - 2y + 5) + (2y^5 + 3y^3 + 7y + 2)$
Arrange in columns of like terms and then add

$$3y^5 + y^4 + 2y^3 - 2y + 5$$
$$\underline{2y^5 + 3y^3 + 7y + 2}$$

$$5y^5 + y^4 + 5y^3 + 5y + 7$$

2. B
$(x^2 - 2)(3x^2 - 3x + 7) = ?$

$= x^2(3x^2 - 3x + 7) - 2(3x^2 - 3x + 7)$

$= x^2(3x^2) + x^2(-3x) + x^2(7) - 2(3x^2) - 2(-3x) - 2(7)$ (6 terms)

$= 3x^4 - 3x^3 + 7x^2 - 6x^2 + 6x - 14$

$= 3x^4 - 3x^3 + (7 - 6)x^2 + 6x - 14$

$= 3x^4 - 3x^3 + x^2 + 6x - 14$

3. C
First, we need to write two equations separately:

$4x - y = 5$ (I)

$x + 2y = 8$ (II) ... Here, we can use two ways to solve the system. One is substitution method, the other one is linear elimination method:

1. Substitution Method:

Equation (I) gives us that $y = 4x - 5$. We insert this value of y into equation (II):

$x + 2(4x - 5) = 8$

$x + 8x - 10 = 8$

$9x - 10 = 8$

$9x = 18$

$x = 2$

Knowing $x = 2$, we can find the value of y by inserting $x = 2$ into either of the equations. Let us choose equation (I):

$4(2) - y = 5$

$8 - y = 5$

$8 - 5 = y$

$y = 3$ → solution is (2, 3)

2. Linear Elimination Method:

$2 \bullet /\ 4x - y = 5$ ... by multiplying equation (I) by 2, we see that -2y will form; and y terms

$\quad x + 2y = 8$ ... will be eliminated when summed with +2y in equation (II):

$2 \bullet /\ 4x - y = 5$

$+\quad \underline{x + 2y = 8}$

$\quad 8x - 2y = 10$

$+\ \underline{x + 2y = 8}$ ... Summing side-by-side:

$8x + x - 2y + 2y = 10 + 8$ ... -2y and +2y cancel

$9x = 18$

$x = 2$

By knowing $x = 2$, we can find the value of y by inserting $x = 2$ into either of the equations. Let us choose equation (I):

$4(2) - y = 5$

$8 - y = 5$

$8 - 5 = y$

$y = 3$ → solution is (2, 3)

4. B
Write similar terms together:

$3x^3 + 2x^2 + 5x - 7 + 4x^2 - 5x + 2 - 3x^3$

$= 3x^3 - 3x^3 + 2x^2 + 4x^2 + 5x - 5x - 7 + 2$

$3x^3$ and $-3x^3$, $5x$ and $-5x$ cancel

$= 6x^2 - 5$

5. A
Following the x values 1.8, -1.8 and -0.6; we need to find the corresponding y values that give the values of the function at those points:

$f(1.8) = -2.2$

$f(-1.8) = 0$

$f(-0.6) = 0.5$

$(f(1.8) - f(-1.8)) / f(-0.6) = (-2.2 - 0) / 0.5 = -22/5 = -4.4$

6. B
Finding the x-intercepts of a function means that we need to equate the function to zero and find the roots of the equation:

$(x - 5)^2 - 9 = 9$

$(x - 5)^2 = 9$

$\sqrt{(x - 5)^2} = \sqrt{9}$

$x - 5 = 3 \rightarrow x = 8$

$x - 5 = -3 \rightarrow x = 2$

7. D
First simplify and have x alone and on one side to solve the inequality:

$(2x + 1)/(2x - 1) < 1$

$(2x + 1)/(2x - 1) - 1 < 0$ ... We need to write the left side at the common denominator $2x - 1$:

$(2x + 1)/(2x - 1) - (2x - 1)/(2x - 1) < 0$

$(2x + 1 - 2x + 1)/(2x - 1) < 0$ ... $2x$ and $-2x$ terms cancel in the numerator:

$2/(2x - 1) < 0$

2 is a positive number; so,

$2x - 1 < 0$

$2x < 1$

$x < 1/2$ ... This means that x should be smaller than $1/2$ and not equal to $1/2$. This is shown as $(-\infty, 1/2)$.

8. D
To solve the equation, we need the equation in the form $ax^2 + bx + c = 0$.

$(a^2 - b^2)x^2 + 2ax + 1 = 0$ is already in this form.

The quadratic formula to find the roots of a quadratic equation is:

$x_{1,2} = (-b \pm \sqrt{\Delta}) / 2a$ where $\Delta = b^2 - 4ac$ and is called the discriminant of the quadratic equation.

In our question, the equation is $(a^2 - b^2)x^2 + 2ax + 1 = 0$.

By remembering the form $ax^2 + bx + c = 0$: $a = a^2 - b^2$, $b = 2a$, $c = 1$

So, we can find the discriminant first, and then the roots of the equation:

$\Delta = b^2 - 4ac = (2a)^2 - 4(a^2 - b^2) * 1 = 4a^2 - 4a^2 + 4b^2 = 4b^2$

$x_{1,2} = (-b \pm \sqrt{\Delta}) / 2a = (-2a \pm \sqrt{4b^2}) / (2(a^2 - b^2)) = (-2a \pm 2b) / (2(a^2 - b^2))$

$= 2(-a \pm b) / (2(a^2 - b^2))$ ... We can simplify by 2:

$= (-a \pm b) / (a^2 - b^2)$

This means that the roots are,

$x_1 = (-a - b) / (a^2 - b^2)$ ... $a^2 - b^2$ is two square differences:

$x_1 = -(a + b) / ((a - b)(a + b))$ ... $(a + b)$ terms cancel:

$x_1 = -1/(a - b)$

$x_2 = (-a + b) / (a^2 - b^2)$ ... $a^2 - b^2$ is two square differences:

$x_2 = -(a - b) / ((a - b)(a + b))$ ... $(a - b)$ terms cancel:

$x_2 = -1/(a + b)$

9. A
To simplify, remove the parenthesis and see if any terms cancel:

$(a + b)(x + y) + (a - b)(x - y) - (ax + by) = ax + ay + bx + by + ax - ay - bx + by - ax - by$

Writing similar terms together:

$= ax + ax - ax + bx - bx + ay - ay + by + by - by$ ... + terms cancel - terms:

$= ax + by$

10. C
We are asked to add polynomials A + B. By paying attention to the sign distribution; we write the polynomials and operate:

$A + B = (4x^5 - 2x^2 + 3x - 2) + (-3x^4 - 5x^2 - 4x + 5)$

$= 4x^5 - 2x^2 + 3x - 2 - 3x^4 - 5x^2 - 4x + 5$ ... Writing similar terms together:

$= 4x^5 - 3x^4 - 2x^2 - 5x^2 + 3x - 4x - 2 + 5$ ... Operating within similar terms:

$= 4x^5 - 3x^4 - 7x^2 - x + 3$

11. A

$x - y = 11 \rightarrow x = 11 + y$

$xy = 24$

$(11+y)y = -24$

$11y + y^2 = -24$

$y^2 + 11y + 24 = 0$

$y_{1,2} = (-11 \pm \sqrt{121 - 96})/2$

$y_{1,2} = (-11 \pm \sqrt{25})/2$

$y_{1,2} = (-11 \pm 5)/2$

$y_1 = -8$

$y_2 = -3$

$x_1 = 11 + y_1 = 11 - 8 = 3$

$x_2 = 11 + y_2 = 11 - 3 = 8$

12. C

x

$y = x + 1$
$z = x + 2$

$x^2 + y^2 = z^2$

$x^2 + (x + 1)^2 = (x + 2)^2$

$x^2 + x^2 + 2x + 1 = x^2 + 4x + 4$

$x^2 - 2x - 3 = 0$

$x_{1,2} = (2 \pm \sqrt{4 + 12})/2$

$x_{1,2} = (2 \pm 4)/2$

$x = 3$
$y = 4$
$z = 5$

13. A

-x - 7 = -3x - 9

-x + 3x = -9 + 7

2x = -2

x = (-2):2

x = -1

14. C

3(x + 2) - 2(1 - x) = 4x + 5

3x + 6 - 2 + 2x = 4x + 5

5x + 4 = 4x + 5

5x - 4x = 5 - 4

x = 1

15. B

Recall that if two lines are parallel, they have the same slope. If we have an equation in the form of
y = mx + b; m represents the slope of the line. The slope of line y = 3x + 2 is 3. So, we are searching for the choice that contains a slope value that is <u>not</u> 3:

    a. 3y = 9x - 8 → y = 3x - 8/3 → m = 3
    b. y = -2x + 2 → m = -2; This slope is not equal to 3.
    c. y = 3x + 5 → m = 3
    d. -4y = 5 - 12x → 4y = 12x - 5 → y = 3x - 5/4 → m = 3

16. A

my age / my brother's age = 2/5
my brother's age / our cousin's age = 3/7

Notice that my brother's age is the common variable and the corresponding numbers are 5 and 3. Then, we use lcm of 3 and 5. Let us say that my brother's age = 15k.

Consequently:

my age / 15k = 2/5 → my age = 6k

15k / our cousin's age = 3/7 → our cousin's age = 35k

The rate of my age to my cousin's age = 6k / 35k = 6/35

17. C
Recall that
$a^3 - b^3 = (a - b)(a^2 + ab + b^2)$ → $8x^3 - 1$

$= (2x - 1)(4x^2 + 2x + 1) ((8x^3 + 1) / (12x^2 + 6x + 3)) : ((2x - 1) / (x + 1))$

$= (((2x - 1)(4x^2 + 2x + 1)) / (3(4x^2 + 2x + 1)))^* ((x + 1) / (2x - 1))$

Simplifying the same terms in the numerator and denominator:

$= (x + 1) / 3$

18. B
We have two variables: the price of a t-shirt and a pair of pants; and we have two situations given about them. We need to set two equations and solve them for the variables. Then, we are asked to find the difference.

Let us call the price of a t-shirt by a, and the price of a pair of pants by b:

If John buys 4 t-shirts and 5 pair of pants, he pays
$51 → 4a + 5b = 51

If he buys 7 t-shirts and 3 pair of pants, then he pays
$49 → 7a + 3b = 49

4a + 5b = 51

7a + 3b = 49

We have two paths to follow: substitution or elimination. Here, since extracting a or b from either equation results in fractions; it is easier to choose elimination:

-3/ 4a + 5b = 51

5/ 7a + 3b = 49

-12a - 15b = -153

<u>35a + 15b = 245</u>

    23a = 92

      a = 4

Choosing either of the equations, find b, by inserting a:

4 * 4 + 5b = 51

16 + 5b = 51

5b = 35

b = 7

The difference between a and b is 7 - 4 = 3.

19. D
The simplest way to draw the graph of a linear equation is to insert zero into x and y separately and to obtain two points on the line.

4x - y = 6 is the equation of the line.

If x = 0, y = - 6 → point (0, - 6) is obtained

If y = 0, x = 6/4 = 1.5 → point (1.5, 0) is obtained

Line 4x - y = 6 passes through (0, - 6) and (1.5, 0)

The graph satisfying the condition is given in choice D.

20. D
More than one x value can result in the same y value, but a x value cannot result in different y values in a set of data or a graph to represent a function. Check all answer choices:

    a. {(0, 2), (1, 5), (5, 5), (3, 0)}
    Notice that when x = 0, y = 2; when x = 1 and 5, y = 5

and when x = 3, y = 0. As mentioned above, two different x values can give the same y value but the reverse is not possible for a function. Therefore, x = 1 and x = 5 giving y = 5 is possible for a function; the other pairs already fit function properties.

b. y = 4x² is a function; we can find corresponding y values by inserting any x value. Since this is an even function; f(- x) = f(x).

c. If we have a graph, the easiest way to check whether it represents a function or not is to draw vertical lines, parallel to y-axis. If the line drawn intersects with the graph at more than one point, then it is not a function:

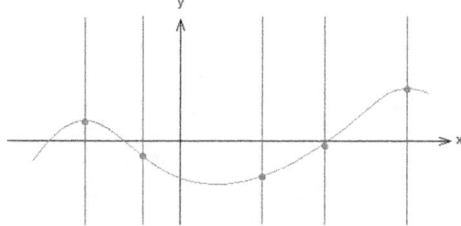

The lines intersect with the graph at only one point, so this is the graph of a function.

d. Applying the same method, we see that vertical lines intersect with the graph at two points.

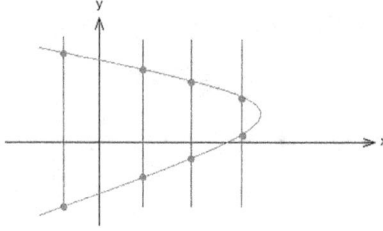

This means that the graph is not a function.

Part III - Functions

1. D
Drawing the graph of a 5th degree polynomial is not a practical way to solve this problem. Instead, remember some properties of polynomial graphs:

Notice that this is an odd degree polynomial. So, two ends of the graph head off in opposite directions. If the leading term is positive; the left end would be down and the right end up. However, the leading term here is $-2x^5$ that is negative. So, the end behavior for this function is up on the left and down on the right.

2. B
We are asked to find the first derivative of function f that is the multiplication of functions g and h:

$f(x) = (x^2 - 2)(x^2 - 2)^3 = (x^2 - 2)^4$

The simple derivation formula of exponential expressions is: $(d/dx)\ x^n = n\,^*x^{n-1}$. However, in this question, the function that is the base of the exponential is a function of x. The general formula should be applied for derivation is:

$(d/dx)\ [a(x)^n] = n * a(x)^{n-1} * a\ '(x)$

$(d/dx)\ [(x^2 - 2)^4] = 4 * (x^2 - 2)^3 * (2x)$

$= 8x(x^2 - 3)^3$

3. C
The antiderivative of a function f is the function that when it is derived, f is obtained. We can find the antiderivative of each term separately and then combine:

The antiderivative of $1/x$ is $\int dx/x = \ln x + C_1$

The antiderivative of x^3 is $\int x^3\ dx = x^4/4 + C_2$

The antiderivative of $\cos x$ is $\int \cos x\ dx = \sin x + C_3$

The overall antiderivative of the expression $1/x + x^3 - \cos x$ is:

$\int (1/x + x^3 - \cos x)\, dx = \ln x + x^4/4 - \sin x + C$ when all constants are collected under "C."

4. D
We know that $a_n = 7^{2n-5}$. Let us calculate a_{n+2}:

$a_{n+2} = 7^{2(n+2)-5} = 7^{2n+4-5} = 7^4 * 7^{2n-5} = 7^4 * a_n$

7^4 times a_n is equal to a_{n+2}.

5. B
Following the parts of the piecewise function, we need to find the values of the given functions by inserting the x values into the corresponding definition:

$x = 1 \rightarrow f(x) = -x/2 \rightarrow f(1) = -1/2$

$x = 3 \rightarrow f(x) = x^3 + 2 \rightarrow f(3) = 3^3 + 2 = 29$

$x = 0 \rightarrow f(x) = -x/2 \rightarrow f(0) = 0$

$x = 2 \rightarrow f(x) = x^3 + 2 \rightarrow f(2) = 2^3 + 2 = 10$

$(f(1) * f(3) - f(0)) / f^2(2) = (-1/2 * 29 - 0) / 10^2$

$= -29/200$

$= -0.145$

6. B
$f(x) = -x$

$g(x) = 2x + 1$

$h(x) = x^2$

$f \circ g \circ h = f(g(h(x)))$

$= f(g(x^2))$

$= f(2x^2 + 1)$
$= -(2x^2 + 1)$

$= -2x^2 - 1$

7. D
$f(x) = 3x + 3$

$f^{-1}(f(x)) = x$

$f^{-1}(3x + 3) = x$

$3x + 3 = t$

$3x = t - 3$

$x = (t - 3)/3$

$f^{-1}(t) = (t - 3)/3$

$f^{-1}(x) = (x - 3)/3$

8. C
$f(x) = (5x - 2)/4$

$f^{-1}(f(x)) = x$

$f^{-1}((5x - 2)/4) = x$

$(5x - 2)/4 = t$

$5x - 2 = 4t$

$5x = 4t + 2$

$x = (4t + 2)/5$

$f^{-1}(t) = (4t + 2)/5$

$f^{-1}(x) = (4x + 2)/5$

9. B
f(x) = 1 - x

f^{-1}(1 - x) = x

1 - x = t

x = 1 - t

f^{-1}(t) = 1 - t

f^{-1}(x) = 1 - x

f^{-1}(1/2) = 1 - 1/2 = 1/2

10. C
First, determine the characteristics of the sequence. Note that the difference between 1st and 2nd terms is 3. However, the difference between 2nd and 3rd terms is 6. So, this is not an arithmetic sequence. The factor between 1st and 2nd term is 2. This factor is 2 for 2nd and 3rd terms as well. So, this is a geometric sequence. The sum formula for a geometric sequence is given by:

$S_n = a_1 (1 - r^n) / (1 - r)$ where S_n is the sum of the terms up to the nth term. We are asked to find the sum up to 10th term. r is the common ratio that is the factor between two successive terms; it is 2 for this question. a_1 is the first term of the sequence that is 3 according to the given data. So, inserting these values:

S_n = 3 (1 - 2^{10}) / (1 - 2) = 3 (-1023) / (-1) = 3 * 1023 = 3069

Note that the manual way to solve this problem is to write the whole sequence up to the requested term and sum. However, this may not always be practical.

11. B
Recall the identity: $\log_a(b/c) = \log_a b - \log_a c$:

$\log_2(3x + 11) - \log_2(x + 2) = 2$

$\log_2((3x + 11) / (x + 2)) = 2$

Let us make both sides the power of 2 to use the identity: $a^{\log_a b} = b$:

$2^{\log_2 ((3x + 11) / (x + 2))} = 2^2$

$(3x + 11) / (x + 2) = 4$

$3x + 11 = 4x + 8$

$11 - 8 = 4x - 3x$

$x = 3$

12. D

This question is about recognizing trigonometric functions. We are searching for the maximum value of the function given. This depends on the minimum value of $\sin(2\pi t / 31)$ since it is the subtracted term in the expression. Remember that sinx changes between -1 and 1; so its minimum value is -1. Then;

$M(t)_{max} = 50{,}000 - 350(-1)$

$= 50{,}000 + 350$

$= \$50{,}350$

13. C

The x values are the domain and the y values are the range. The domain of this set of data is {- 5, 2, 4, 7, 12} and the range is {- 3, 4, 9, 15, 18}.

14. C

There are two points important in this question:

1. The term inside the square root cannot be smaller than zero which limits the range.

2. There are x values that make the denominator zero which make the function undefined. So, these values should be eliminated.

$\sqrt{(x - 5)} / (x + 5)$

x - 5 ≥ 0 → x ≥ 5. Then, x < 5 should be eliminated.

x + 5 ≠ 0 → x ≠ -5. Then, x = -5 should be eliminated.

Notice that -5 is already in x < 5. So, only excluding x < 5 values will be sufficient.

The domain of the function is: [5, +∞)

15. A

The rate of change that is the velocity, is the distance change by time. Observing that the graph is linear, find the rate of change by taking any two points and calculating the slope:

rate of change = distance change / time change

Let us choose (12, 31) and (24, 46):

rate of change = (46 - 31) / (24 - 12)

= 15 / 12 = 1.25 m/s

Part IV - Calculus

1. A
Remember the integral of x^a is found by:
$x^{a+1} / (a + 1)$

Constant coefficients inside the integral can be directly taken out. So,

$\int_{-3}^{2} 2x - 3 \, dx = 2(x - 3 + 1 / (-3 + 1)) \Big|_{-3}^{2} = -x - 2 \Big|_{-3}^{2}$

= -(2-2 - (-3)-2) = -(1/4 - 1/9)

= -5/36

2. A
The fundamental theorem of calculus mentions that, with f continuous on [a, b]:

If $F(x) = \int_a^x f(t)dt \rightarrow F'(x) = f(x)$

Notice that the limits of the integral in the question need to be changed to make x the upper limit:

$G(x) = \int_x^{\pi/4} \cos^2 3x\, dx = -\int_{\pi/4}^x \cos^2 3x\, dx$

We see that G'(x) = -f(x).

Since f(x) = -cos²3x, G'(x) = -cos²3x.

G'(π/6) = - cos²(3 * π/6) = -cos²(π/2) = 0

3. C
Let us expand the asked expression:

$\int_{-1}^3 (4g(x) - 5f(x))dx = \int_{-1}^3 4g(x)dx - \int_{-1}^3 5f(x)dx$

Notice that the limits of the integrals change from -1 to 3. In the given integrals, they change from -1 to 3 for f(x), but from 3 to -1 for g(x). We can do the following shifting:

$\int_3^{-1} g(x)dx = 8 \rightarrow \int_{-1}^3 g(x)dx = -8$

So:

$\int_{-1}^3 4g(x)dx - \int_{-1}^3 5f(x)dx = 4\int_{-1}^3 g(x)dx - 5\int_{-1}^3 f(x)dx$

= 4(-8) - 5(-15) = - 32 + 75 = 43

4. C
The first derivative of a function is the slope of the tangent line to the function. If the slope of this line is positive, then the line shows an increasing linear correspondence which means that the function is increasing as well. On the contrary; if the first derivative is negative, the slope of the

tangent line is negative; then, it is decreasing linearly. So, the function is decreasing.

The second derivative of a function tells us if the first derivative of the function is increasing or decreasing. If the second derivative is positive, then the first derivative is increasing, so the slope of the tangent line is increasing. Consequently; the graph of f is concave up shaped. On the other hand; if the second derivative is negative, then the first derivative is decreasing, so the slope of the tangent line is decreasing. Consequently; the graph of f is concave down shaped.

5. D

Recall that the Taylor Series for $1/(1-x)$ is:

$$1/(1-x) = 1 + x^2 + x^3 + x^4 + \ldots$$

$$= \sum_{n=0}^{\infty} x^n$$

for $-1 < x < 1$. This interval is important. We need to find the x value that satisfy $1/(1-x) = 5/4$. If x is within $-1 < x < 1$, we can proceed:

$1/(1-x) = 5/4$

$5 - 5x = 4$

$5x = 1$

$x = 1/5$

x is found to be within the interval, so we can continue solving. Let us sum the first 5 terms of the series. This means that n starts by 0, ends by 4 because n = 0 gives the first term:

$$1/(1-x) = 1 + x^2 + x^3 + x^4 + \ldots$$

$$= \sum_{n=0}^{\infty} x^n$$

$$= \sum_{n=0}^{4} (1/5)^n = (1/5)^0 + (1/5)^1 + (1/5)^2 + (1/5)^3 + (1/5)^4$$

$= 1 + 1/5 + 1/25 + 1/125 + 1/625 = 1.2496$

Rounding to the nearest hundredths:

$1.2496 = 1.25$ that is the exact value of $5/4 = 1.25$

6. A

Note that the flow rate of water is V'(t) that is the volume change by time. We are asked to find the height change by time: h'(t). Since the radius is constant, only volume and height depend on time.

Remembering the volume of a cylinder:

$V = \pi r^2 h$

$V(t) = \pi r^2 h(t)$

$(d/dt) V(t) = \pi r^2 (d/dt) h(t)$

$V' = \pi r^2 h'$

Inserting the given values:

$8 = \pi * 2^2 * h'$

$h' = 2/\pi$

7. C

First, reorganize the differential equation to prepare for integration:

$dy/dx = x^3/y^2$ ... by cross multiplication:

$y^2 * dy = x^3 * dx$

$\int y^2 * dy = \int x^3 * dx$

$y^3/3 = x^4/4 + C$ ... It is important not to forget the constant C for indefinite integration.

$y^3 = 3x^4/4 + 3C$

$y = \sqrt[3]{(3x^4/4 + 3C)}$

8. B
The derivative of a function as limit is found by:

$f'(x) = \lim\limits_{x \to 0} (f(x + \Delta x) - f(x)) / \Delta x$

Here, $f(x) = 3x^2 - 2x + 7$

→ $f(x + \Delta x) = 3(x + \Delta x)^2 - 2(x + \Delta x) + 7 = 3x^2 + 6x\Delta x + (\Delta x)^2 - 2x - 2\Delta x + 7$

$f'(x) = \lim\limits_{\Delta x \to 0} (f(x + \Delta x) - f(x)) / \Delta x$

$= \lim\limits_{\Delta x \to 0} (3x^2 + 6x\Delta x + (\Delta x)^2 - 2x - 2\Delta x + 7 - 3x^2 + 2x - 7) / \Delta x$

$= \lim\limits_{\Delta x \to 0} (6x\Delta x + (\Delta x)^2 - 2\Delta x) / \Delta x$

$= \lim\limits_{\Delta x \to 0} (6x + \Delta x - 2)$

$= 6x - 2$

9. A
The fundamental theorem of calculus mentions that, with f continuous on [a, b]:

If $F(x) = \int_a^x f(t)dt$ → $F'(x) = f(x)$

$F(x) = \int_4^x x^5 dx$, we are asked to find $F'(3)$

Since $f(x) = x^5$, $F'(x) = x^5$

$F'(3) = 3^5 = 243$

10. D
The local minimum and maximum of a function are found by the second derivative test. First, we need to take the first

derivative of the function:

f(x) = 6x³ - 36x + 23

f '(x) = 18x² - 36

Let us check if there are any x values to make f ' zero:

18x² - 36 = 0 → x² = 2 → x = √2 and x = - √2

Then: f(√2) = 0 and f(- √2) = 0

Next step is to calculate f ''(x) and insert √2 and - √2 to check if these values make the second derivative positive or negative:

f ''(x) = 36x

f ''(√2) = 36√2 > 0 ... Then, (√2, 36√2) is a local minimum

f ''(- √2) = - 36√2 < 0 ... Then, (- √2, - 36√2) is a local maximum

Part V - Geometry and Measurement

1. B
In the question, we have a right triangle formed inside the circle. We are asked to find the length of the hypotenuse of this triangle. We can find the other two sides of the triangle by using circle properties:

The diameter of the circle is equal to 12 cm. The legs of the right triangle are the radii of the circle; so they are 6 cm long.

Using the Pythagorean Theorem:

(Hypotenuse)² = (Adjacent Side)² + (Opposite Side)²

x² = r² + r²

x² = 6² + 6²

x² = 72

$x = \sqrt{72}$

$x = 8.48$

2. B

We see that there are three squares forming a right triangle in the middle. Two of the squares have the areas 81 m² and 144 m². If we denote their sides a and b respectively:

$a^2 = 81$ and $b^2 = 144$. The length, which is asked, is the hypotenuse; a and b are the opposite and adjacent sides of the right angle. By using the Pythagorean Theorem, we can find the value of the asked side:

Pythagorean Theorem:

$(Hypotenuse)^2 = (Opposite\ Side)^2 + (Adjacent\ Side)^2$

$h^2 = a^2 + b^2$

$a^2 = 81$ and $b^2 = 144$ are given. So,

$h^2 = 81 + 144$

$h^2 = 225$

$h = 15$ m

3.

We reflect points A, B, C and D against the mirror line m at right angle and we connect the new points A', B', C' and D'.

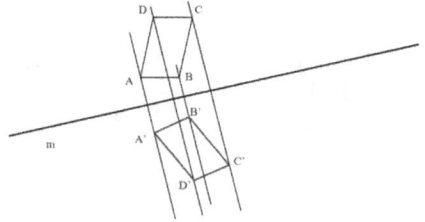

4.
We reflect the center O against the mirror line m at right angle and we use a compass to draw the circle with the same radius as the original circle.

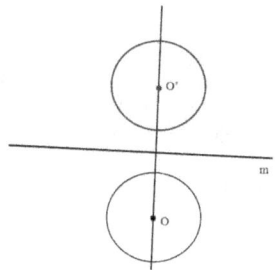

5. C
Comparing respective sides, ABCD, KLMN, WXYZ are similar.

6. C
The class can be shown by set E. Let us say, set D represents dancing lessons, and set S represents singing lessons.

8 students take only dancing lessons: s(D\S) = 8

5 students take both dancing and singing lessons: s(D∩S) = 5

The number of students taking singing lessons:
s(S) = 2 * 8 - 1 = 15

s(S) = s(S\D) + s(D∩S) and also s(D) = s(D\S) + s(D∩S)

4 students take neither of these courses: s(E) - s(D ∪ S) = 4

s(D ∪ S) can be found by s(D\S) + s(S) or s(S\D) + s(D)

We are asked to find s(E):

s(E) = 4 + s(D\S) + s(S) = 4 + 8 + 15 = 27

7. B
The interior angles of a triangle sum up to 180°:

(2x + 5) + (6x) + (3x - 23) = 180

$11x - 18 = 180$

$11x = 198$

$x = 18°$

The largest angle is $6x = 6 * 18 = 108°$

The supplementary of an angle is the angle which plus the angle gives $180°$. Then, the supplementary of $108°$ is:

$180 - 108 = 72°$

8. D
In the right triangle above, AB and BC are the legs and AC is the hypotenuse. For side lengths, Pythagorean Theorem is applied:

$|AB|^2 + |BC|^2 = |AC|^2$

Let us say that $|BC| = x$. Then, $|AB| = 2x$:

$(2x)^2 + x^2 = 15^2$

$5x^2 = 225$

$x^2 = 45$

$x = \sqrt{45} = 3\sqrt{5}$ cm

$|AB| = 2x \rightarrow |AB| = 6\sqrt{5}$ cm

9. C
The perimeter of an equilateral triangle with 9 cm. sides will be $= 9 + 9 + 9 = 27$ cm.

10. A
The question is to find the perimeter of a shape made by merging a square and a semi circle. Perimeter = 3 sides of the square + ½ circumference of the circle.
$= (3 \times 5) + ½(5 \pi)$
$= 15 + 2.5 \pi$
Perimeter = 22.85 cm

11. B
The general form of conic equation is:
$Ax^2 + Cy^2 + Dx + Ey + F = 0; B = 0$

Practice Test Questions 1

Since A = C in the given equation in the question; this is a circle or one of its degenerate forms. We need to re-organise the formula to obtain the known circle equation:

$x^2 + y^2 - 2x + 6y + 10 = 0$

$x^2 - 2x \underline{+ 1 - 1} + y^2 + 6y \underline{+ 9 - 9} + 10 = 0$

$(x - 1)^2 + (y + 3)^2 - 10 + 10 = 0$

$(x - 1)^2 + (y + 3)^2 = 0$

The right-hand side of the equation stands for r^2; but since it is zero, the radius of the circle is zero, meaning that it represents a point; that is the equation of the point (1, -3). So the range of the graph is -3.

12. D
Parallel lines have equal slopes. We first need to reorganize the line equations to obtain the form y = mx + b, where m is the slope:

$6y - x - 7 = 0$

$6y = x + 7$

$y = (1/6)x + 7/6 \rightarrow m = 1/6$

$ay = 3x + 5$

$y = (3/a)x + 5/a \rightarrow m = 3/a$

Since the slopes are equal:

$1/6 = 3/a \rightarrow a = 18$

13. C
At first glance, the given shape is not a shape that we are accustomed to see. However, remembering Cavalieri's principle, we notice that this shape has properties in common with the rectangle below:

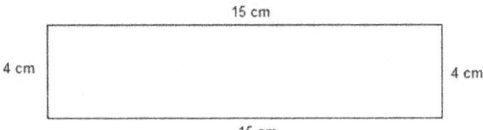

According to Cavalieri; if two shapes have the same height and matching widths everywhere along the height, the shapes have the same area. So, the area of the shape in the question is equal to the area of the rectangle above; that is $4 * 15 = 60$ cm^2.

14. D
The Euclidian geometry was disproven by Nikolai Lobachevsky in 1830s.

15. C
Euclidian geometry supports parallel geometry. On the contrary, Non-Euclidian geometry is the study of geometry with curved spaces that is elliptic and hyperbolic geometry. In elliptic geometry; the inner angles of a triangle do not sum up to 1800; the sum is equal to 1800 plus the area of the triangle. In hyperbolic geometry; the sum is equal to 1800 minus the area of the triangle. non-Euclidian geometry inspires from the shape of the world: If two meridians are selected; both intersect with the equator by 900. There is also a vertex angle in the pole. So, the inner angles sum up to 90 + 90 + vertex pole which is higher than 1800.

Another example; a person walks 10 m south, 10 m west and then 10 m north. He sees that he is where he started moving. Normally, we would say that he would be 10 m east from the starting point. Think that he is on the North Pole. If he goes 10 m down, 10 m west and then 10 m north, he is again on the pole.

Part VI - Statistics and Probability

1. A
There are 8 balls in the bag in total. It is important that two balls are taken out of the bag one by one. We can first take the blue then the white, or first white, then the blue. So, we will have two possibilities to be summed up. Since the balls are taken consecutively, we should be careful with the total number of balls for each case:

First blue, then white ball:

There are 3 blue balls; so, having a blue ball is 3/8 possible. Then, we have 7 balls left in the bag. The possibility to have a white ball is 1/7.

P = (3/8) * (1/7) = 3/56

First white, then blue ball:

There is only 1 white ball; so, having a white ball is 1/8 possible. Then, we have 7 balls left in the bag. The possibility to have a blue ball is 3/7.

P = (1/8) * (3/7) = 3/56

Overall probability is:

3/56 + 3/56 = 3/28

2. B
First add all the numbers 100 + 1050 + 320 + 600 + 150 = 2220. Then divide by 5 (the number of data provided) = 2220/5 = 444.

3. A
Here, we can use binomial distribution - probability mass function:

$C(n, x) * p^x * q^{n-x}$

where n is the number of hits, x is the successful number of hits, p is the success probability and q is the failure probability. Since the success probability is 1/6, failure probability is 1 - 1/6 = 5/6:

$C(n, x) * p^x * q^{n-x}$ = C(6, 4) * (1/6)^4 * (5/6)^2 = (6! / (2! * 4!)) * (25 / 6^6) = 0.008

4. A
Probability that the 1st ball is red: 4/11

Probability the 2nd ball is green: 5/10

Combined probability is 4/11 * 5/10 = 20/110 = 2/11

5. B

80 out of 120 expect to eat out 5 days next month. This information gives the proportion of people expecting to eat out to total number of people. However, not all employees participated the survey; so we accept that the random sample represents all employees:

If 80 out of 120 expect to eat out next month, how many employees out of 450 expect to eat out next month?

450 * 80 / 120 = 300 employees

6. D

First arrange the numbers in a numerical sequence - 1,2,3,4,5,6,7,8,9, 10. Then find the middle number or numbers. The middle numbers are 5 and 6. The median = 5 + 6/2 = 11/2 = 5.5

7. B

The most occurring number in the series (7, 9, 10, 13, 11, 7, 9, 19, 12, 11, 9, 7, 9, 10, 11) is 9.

8. D

Assume that the first book chosen is red. Since we need to choose the second book in green or blue, there are 10 possible books to be chosen out of 15 - 1(that is the red book chosen first) = 14 books. There are equal number of books in each color, so the results will be the same if we think that blue or green book is the first book.

So, the probability will be 10/14 = 5/7.

9. B

Ignoring the order means this is a combination problem, not permutation. The reader will choose 3 books out of 4. So,

C(4, 3) = 4! / (3! * (4 - 3)!) = 4! / (3! * 1!) = 4

There are 4 different ways.

Ignoring the order means this is a combination problem, not permutation. The reader will choose 3 books out of 4. So,

C(4, 3) = 4! / (3! * (4 - 3)!) = 4! / (3! * 1!) = 4

There are 4 different ways.

10. C

The expected value is found by the formula:

$$E(x) = \mu = \sum_{i=1}^{m} x_i * P(x = x_i).$$ It is

important to check that the probabilities given in the question sum up to 1; they do for this question.

So, E(x) = µ = 0 * 0.30 + 1 * 0.25 + 2 * 0.20 + 3 * 0.12 + 4 * 0.10 + 5 * 0.03 = 1.56

Practice Test Questions Set 2 (More Difficult)

The questions below are not the same as you will find on the NYSTCE® Mathematics test- that would be too easy! And nobody knows what the questions will be and they change all the time. Below are general questions that cover the same subject areas as the NYSTCE® Mathematics test. So, while the format and exact wording of the questions may differ slightly, and change from year to year, if you can answer the questions below, you will have no problem with the NYSTCE Mathematics test.

For the best results, take these Practice Test Questions as if it were the real exam. Set aside time when you will not be disturbed, and a location that is quiet and free of distractions. Read the instructions carefully, read each question carefully, and answer to the best of your ability.
Use the bubble answer sheets provided. When you have completed the Practice Questions, check your answer against the Answer Key and read the explanation provided.

Do not attempt more than one set of practice test questions in one day. After completing the first practice test, wait two or three days before attempting the second set of questions.

Part I - Number and Quantity

1. Ⓐ Ⓑ Ⓒ Ⓓ 11. Ⓐ Ⓑ Ⓒ Ⓓ
2. Ⓐ Ⓑ Ⓒ Ⓓ 12. Ⓐ Ⓑ Ⓒ Ⓓ
3. Ⓐ Ⓑ Ⓒ Ⓓ 13. Ⓐ Ⓑ Ⓒ Ⓓ
4. Ⓐ Ⓑ Ⓒ Ⓓ 14. Ⓐ Ⓑ Ⓒ Ⓓ
5. Ⓐ Ⓑ Ⓒ Ⓓ 15. Ⓐ Ⓑ Ⓒ Ⓓ
6. Ⓐ Ⓑ Ⓒ Ⓓ 16. Ⓐ Ⓑ Ⓒ Ⓓ
7. Ⓐ Ⓑ Ⓒ Ⓓ 17. Ⓐ Ⓑ Ⓒ Ⓓ
8. Ⓐ Ⓑ Ⓒ Ⓓ 18. Ⓐ Ⓑ Ⓒ Ⓓ
9. Ⓐ Ⓑ Ⓒ Ⓓ 19. Ⓐ Ⓑ Ⓒ Ⓓ
10. Ⓐ Ⓑ Ⓒ Ⓓ 20. Ⓐ Ⓑ Ⓒ Ⓓ

Part II - Algebra

1. Ⓐ Ⓑ Ⓒ Ⓓ   11. Ⓐ Ⓑ Ⓒ Ⓓ
2. Ⓐ Ⓑ Ⓒ Ⓓ   12. Ⓐ Ⓑ Ⓒ Ⓓ
3. Ⓐ Ⓑ Ⓒ Ⓓ   13. Ⓐ Ⓑ Ⓒ Ⓓ
4. Ⓐ Ⓑ Ⓒ Ⓓ   14. Ⓐ Ⓑ Ⓒ Ⓓ
5. Ⓐ Ⓑ Ⓒ Ⓓ   15. Ⓐ Ⓑ Ⓒ Ⓓ
6. Ⓐ Ⓑ Ⓒ Ⓓ   16. Ⓐ Ⓑ Ⓒ Ⓓ
7. Ⓐ Ⓑ Ⓒ Ⓓ   17. Ⓐ Ⓑ Ⓒ Ⓓ
8. Ⓐ Ⓑ Ⓒ Ⓓ   18. Ⓐ Ⓑ Ⓒ Ⓓ
9. Ⓐ Ⓑ Ⓒ Ⓓ   19. Ⓐ Ⓑ Ⓒ Ⓓ
10. Ⓐ Ⓑ Ⓒ Ⓓ   20. Ⓐ Ⓑ Ⓒ Ⓓ

Part III - Functions

1. Ⓐ Ⓑ Ⓒ Ⓓ
2. Ⓐ Ⓑ Ⓒ Ⓓ
3. Ⓐ Ⓑ Ⓒ Ⓓ
4. Ⓐ Ⓑ Ⓒ Ⓓ
5. Ⓐ Ⓑ Ⓒ Ⓓ
6. Ⓐ Ⓑ Ⓒ Ⓓ
7. Ⓐ Ⓑ Ⓒ Ⓓ
8. Ⓐ Ⓑ Ⓒ Ⓓ
9. Ⓐ Ⓑ Ⓒ Ⓓ
10. Ⓐ Ⓑ Ⓒ Ⓓ
11. Ⓐ Ⓑ Ⓒ Ⓓ
12. Ⓐ Ⓑ Ⓒ Ⓓ
13. Ⓐ Ⓑ Ⓒ Ⓓ
14. Ⓐ Ⓑ Ⓒ Ⓓ
15. Ⓐ Ⓑ Ⓒ Ⓓ

Part IV - Calculus

1. Ⓐ Ⓑ Ⓒ Ⓓ
2. Ⓐ Ⓑ Ⓒ Ⓓ
3. Ⓐ Ⓑ Ⓒ Ⓓ
4. Ⓐ Ⓑ Ⓒ Ⓓ
5. Ⓐ Ⓑ Ⓒ Ⓓ
6. Ⓐ Ⓑ Ⓒ Ⓓ
7. Ⓐ Ⓑ Ⓒ Ⓓ
8. Ⓐ Ⓑ Ⓒ Ⓓ
9. Ⓐ Ⓑ Ⓒ Ⓓ
10. Ⓐ Ⓑ Ⓒ Ⓓ

Part V - Geometry and Measurement

1. Ⓐ Ⓑ Ⓒ Ⓓ   11. Ⓐ Ⓑ Ⓒ Ⓓ
2. Ⓐ Ⓑ Ⓒ Ⓓ   12. Ⓐ Ⓑ Ⓒ Ⓓ
3. Ⓐ Ⓑ Ⓒ Ⓓ   13. Ⓐ Ⓑ Ⓒ Ⓓ
4. Ⓐ Ⓑ Ⓒ Ⓓ   14. Ⓐ Ⓑ Ⓒ Ⓓ
5. Ⓐ Ⓑ Ⓒ Ⓓ   15. Ⓐ Ⓑ Ⓒ Ⓓ
6. Ⓐ Ⓑ Ⓒ Ⓓ
7. Ⓐ Ⓑ Ⓒ Ⓓ
8. Ⓐ Ⓑ Ⓒ Ⓓ
9. Ⓐ Ⓑ Ⓒ Ⓓ
10. Ⓐ Ⓑ Ⓒ Ⓓ

Part VI - Statistics and Probability

1. Ⓐ Ⓑ Ⓒ Ⓓ
2. Ⓐ Ⓑ Ⓒ Ⓓ
3. Ⓐ Ⓑ Ⓒ Ⓓ
4. Ⓐ Ⓑ Ⓒ Ⓓ
5. Ⓐ Ⓑ Ⓒ Ⓓ
6. Ⓐ Ⓑ Ⓒ Ⓓ
7. Ⓐ Ⓑ Ⓒ Ⓓ
8. Ⓐ Ⓑ Ⓒ Ⓓ
9. Ⓐ Ⓑ Ⓒ Ⓓ
10. Ⓐ Ⓑ Ⓒ Ⓓ

Part I - Number and Quantity

1. If A = 2/7 + 4/9 + 6/11, what is 16/7 + 22/9 - 5/11 equal to in terms of A?

    a. A + 3
    b. A + 4
    c. 2A + 3
    d. 2A + 6

2. Simplify the following expression in rational number form:

($\sqrt{4/9}$ * 3/8) / (($^3\sqrt{125}$ / $^4\sqrt{81}$) / 4 - 1/12).

    a. 1/2
    b. 3/4
    c. 4/3
    d. 2

3. What is the result of the expression
($i^{18} - i^5 + 4i^{162} - i^{39}$) / ($i^2 - 1$) ?

    b. 2
    b. 5/2
    c. 7/2
    d. 5

4. We are given that $A = \begin{bmatrix} 1 & 4 \\ 1 & 3 \end{bmatrix}$ and $B = \begin{bmatrix} 2 & 2 \\ 5 & 1 \end{bmatrix}$

Find the X matrix that satisfies A * X = B.

  a. $\begin{bmatrix} 4 & -2 \\ -3 & 0 \end{bmatrix}$
  b. $\begin{bmatrix} 3 & -2 \\ -3 & 1 \end{bmatrix}$
  c. $\begin{bmatrix} 2 & -2 \\ -3 & 3 \end{bmatrix}$
  d. $\begin{bmatrix} 14 & -2 \\ -3 & 1 \end{bmatrix}$

5. Mary deposits $1,000 into an investment account with annual rate of 15% and she regularly invests $1,000 every year for 5 years. How much more money will she have at the end of 5 years? Round your answer to the nearest integer.

    a. $855
    b. $1,534
    c. $2,754
    d. $5,753

6. $\sqrt[4]{2 * \sqrt[3]{4}} * \sqrt[3]{\sqrt{8}} = \sqrt[6]{4 * \sqrt[2]{2^{x+1}}}$ is given. Find the value of x.

    a. 2
    b. 3
    c. 5
    d. 6

7.

100 km/h   80 km/h
⇒   ⇐

A   B   C   D

Two vehicles travelling at 100 km/h and 80 km/h start moving towards one another from cities A and C. When they start moving simultaneously, they meet in city B. If the vehicle with less velocity moved towards city D, two vehicles would meet in city D. Find the ratio |CD| / |BC|.

    a. 5
    b. 6
    c. 8
    d. 9

8. 120 ÷ (6 + 12 x 2)

    a. 150

    b. 40

    c. 6

    d. 4

9. Estimate 46,227 + 101,032

    a. 14,700

    b. 147,000

    c. 14,700,000

    d. 104,700

10. The total expense of building a fence around a square-shaped field is $2000 at a rate of $5 per meter. What is the length of one side?

    a. 40 meters

    b. 80 meters

    c. 100 meters

    d. 320 meters

11. A motorcycle travelling 90 mph accelerates to pass a truck. Five seconds later, the motorcycle is going 120 mph. Calculate the motorcycles' acceleration.

    a. 6 mph/second

    b. 10 mph/second

    c. 15 mph/second

    d. 20 mph/second

12. The space station travels 1000 meters in 5 seconds. How fast is it travelling?

    a. 100 meters/second

    b. 300 meters/second

    c. 200 meter/second

    d. 50 meters/second

13. How much force is needed to accelerate a car weighing 2,000 kg, at a rate of 3 m/s^2?

    a. 2000 N

    b. 4000 N

    c. 6000 N

    d. 5000 N

14. How much force is needed to accelerate a car weighing 200 kg to 5 m/s^2?

    a. 800 N

    b. 1000 N

    c. 1200 N

    d. 1400 N

15. Using the factoring method, solve the quadratic equation: $2x^2 - 3x = 0$

    a. 0 and 1.5

    b. 1.5 and 2

    c. 2 and 2.5

    d. 0 and 2

16. Using the quadratic formula, solve the quadratic equation: $x^2 - 9x + 14 = 0$

   a. 2 and 7
   b. -2 and 7
   c. -7 and -2
   d. -7 and 2

17. Factor the polynomial $9x^2 - 6x + 12$.

   a. $3(x^2 - 2x + 9)$
   b. $3(3x^2 - 3x + 4)$
   c. $9(x^2 - 3x + 3)$
   d. $3(3x^2 - 2x + 4)$

18. Factor the polynomial $x^3y^3 - x^2y^8$.

   a. $x^2y^3(x - y^5)$
   b. $x^3y^3(1 - y^5)$
   c. $x^2y^2(x - y^6)$
   d. $xy^3(x - y^5)$

19. A rocket travels 3000 meters in 5 seconds. How fast is it travelling?

   a. 100 m/sec
   b. 200 m/sec
   c. 500 m/sec
   d. 600 m/sec

20. A car starts from standing stop and in 10 seconds is travelling 20/meters per second. What is the acceleration?

    a, 0.5 m/sec²
    b. 1.5 m/sec²
    c. 1 m/sec²
    d. 2 m/sec²

Part II - Algebra

1. $(3y^5 - 2y + y^4 + 2y^3 + 5) - (2y^5 + 3y^3 + 2 + 7y) =$

    a. $y^5 + y^4 - y^3 - 9y + 3$
    b. $y^5 + y^4 - y^3 - 7y + 2$
    c. $y^3 + y^4 - y^2 - 9y + 3$
    d. $y^2 + y^4 - 2y^3 - 3y + 3$

2. Add $-3x^2 + 2x + 6$ and $-x^2 - x - 1$.

    a. $-2x^2 + x + 5$
    b. $-4x^2 + x + 5$
    c. $-2x^2 + 3x + 5$
    d. $-4x^2 + 3x + 5$

3.

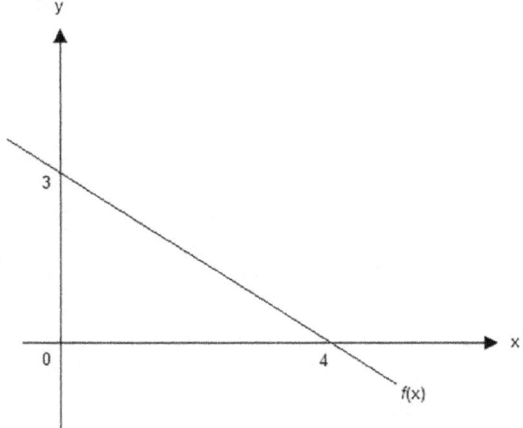

According to the graph of f, find the value of $f^{-1}(2)$.

   a. -1/3
   b. 1/3
   c. 4/3
   d. 8/3

4. Find 2 numbers that sum to 21 and the sum of the squares is 261.

   a. 14 and 7
   b. 15 and 6
   c. 16 and 5
   d. 17 and 4

5.

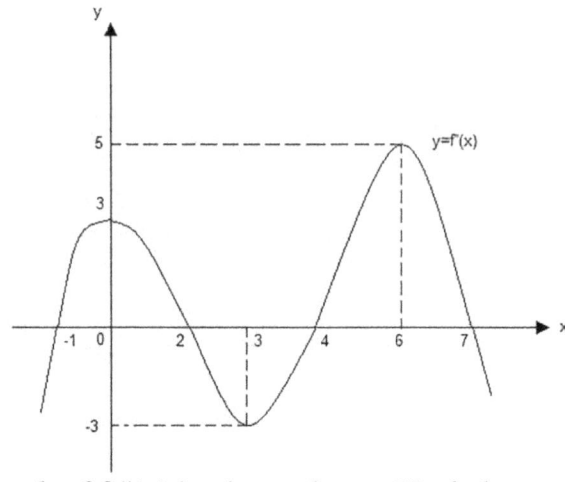

Graph of f "(x) is given above. Find the sum of apsides **of vertexes of function f.**

    a. 3
    b. 5
    c. 8
    d. 12

6. Solve for x if, $10^2 \times 100^2 = 1000^x$

    a. x = 2
    b. x = 3
    c. x = -2
    d. x = 0

7. Given polynomials A = $-2x^4 + x^2 - 3x$, B = $x^4 - x^3 + 5$ and C = $x^4 + 2x^3 + 4x + 5$, find A + B - C.

    a. $x^3 + x^2 + x + 10$
    b. $-3x^3 + x^2 - 7x + 10$
    c. $-2x^4 - 3x^3 + x^2 - 7x$
    d. $-3x^4 + x^3 + \mathbf{2} - 7x$

Practice Test Questions 2

8. Solve the inequality: $(x - 6)^2 \geq x^2 + 12$

    a. $(2, +\infty)$

    b. $[2, +\infty)$

    c. $(-\infty, 2]$

    d. $(12, +\infty)$

9. Multiply $x - 1$ **and** $x^2 + x + 2$.

    a. $x^3 + x - 2$
    b. $x^2 + x - 2$
    c. $x^3 + x^2 - 2$
    d. $x^3 + 2x^2 - 2$

10. The area of a rectangle is 20 cm². If one side increases by 1 cm, and the other by 2 cm, the area of the new rectangle is 35 cm². Find the sides of the original rectangle.

    a. (4,8)

    b. (4,5)

    c. (2.5,8)

    d. b and c

11. Driver B drove his car 20 km/h faster than the driver A, and the driver B travelled 480 km 2 hours before driver A. What was the speed of the driver A?

    a. 70

    b. 80

    c. 60

    d. 90

12. Find the solution for the following linear equation:
$5x/2 = (3x + 24)/6$

    a. -1
    b. 0
    c. 1
    d. 2

13. If a and b are real numbers, solve the following equation: $(a + 2)x - b = -2 + (a + b)x$

    a. -1
    b. 0
    c. 1
    d. 2

14. Find the solution for the following linear equation:
$1 / (4x - 2) = 5/6$

    a. 0.2
    b. 0.4
    c. 0.6
    d. 0.8

15. $(x^2 + x + 3)(2x^2 - 3x + 1) = ?$

    a. $2x^3 - x^2 + 4x - 8x + 1$
    b. $2x^4 - x^2 + 4x + 3$
    c. $2x^3 - x^2 - 8x + 1$
    d. $2x^4 - x^3 + 4x^2 - 8x + 3$

16. The equation of a linear function f is $2y = 4x - 3$. Line d_1 parallel to f is represented by the equation $y = ax + b$, and line d_2 that is perpendicular to f is represented by the equation $y = cx - b$. If lines d_1 and d_2 intersect at point (2, d); find the value of d.

    a. 3/2
    b. 5/2
    c. 3
    d. 5

17. A clock shows the time as a quarter past three. What is the minimum number of minutes where the angle between the hour and minute hands will be 64°?

    a. 13
    b. 25
    c. 37
    d. 45

18. Given
$(1 - 1/2) * (1 - 1/3) * (1 - 1/4) \ldots (1 - 1/(x + 5)) = 1/18$, find the value of x.

    a. 5
    b. 8
    c. 13
    d. 18

19. In a microbiology laboratory, researchers are studying the growth properties of a newly discovered bacterium. It is known that the bacteria exhibits exponential growth. Initially, the researchers put $4 * 10^4$ bacteria into the growth medium. After 120 hours, they measure $1.024 * 10^{15}$ bacteria. Find the growth constant for the bacteria. Round your answer to the nearest tenths place.

    a. 0.1
    b. 0.2
    c. 0.3
    d. 0.4

20. Find the equation of the graph below:

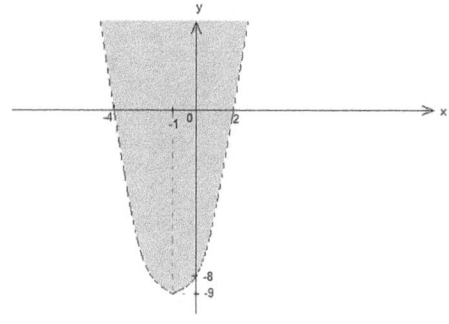

    a. $x^2 + 2x - 8 > 0$
    b. $2x + 8y \geq 0$
    c. $x^2 + 2x - 8 < 0$
    d. $2x - 8y < 0$

Part III - Functions

1. Find the domain of the function $f(x) = \sqrt{(x + 7)} / (x - 3)$.

    a. $[3, 7) \cup (7, +\infty)$
    b. $(-\infty, 3) \cup (3, +\infty)$
    c. $[-7, 3) \cup (3, +\infty)$
    d. $[-7, 3) \cup (3, +\infty]$

2. After finding the first derivative of the function $f(x) = (x^3 + 1) / (x - 2)$, find the remainder of the polynomial division operation.

    a. -9
    b. x + 1
    c. 10
    d. x - 1

3. Check if the given antiderivatives are correct for the given functions.

1) $f(x) = x \sin 3x \rightarrow$ antiderivative = $(-1/3) [x \cos 3x + (1/3) \sin 3x] + C$

2) $f(x) = 1 / (2\sqrt{(3x^3)}) \rightarrow$ antiderivative = $-1 / \sqrt{(3x)} + C$

    a. 1) correct 2) incorrect
    b. 1) correct 2) correct
    c. 1) incorrect 2) incorrect
    d. 1) incorrect 2) correct

4. The initial value for function f is given by f(1) = 3. The general formula of this function is f(x) = x * f(x - 1).

What is the value of f(20)?

    a. 3 * 20!
    b. 20^3
    c. 20 * 21
    d. 600

5. Find g∘f if f(x) = 2x + 5 and g(x) = 5x + 2.

    a. 5x + 5
    b. 10x + 27
    c. 10x + 2
    d. 25x + 25

6. If f(x) = 1 + x^2, find f∘f.

    a. $1 + x^2 + x^4$
    b. $2 + x^2 + x^4$
    c. $2 + x^2$
    d. $1 + x^4$

7. Find $f^{-1}(1/2)$ if f(x) = 1 - x.

    a. 1
    b. 1/2
    c. 1/3
    d. 1/4

8. If $f(x) = 5x$ and $g(x) = 7 - 2x$, find $(f - g)^{-1}(0)$.

   a. 1
   b. 2
   c. 3
   d. 4

9. If $f^{-1}(x) = 2x$, find $f(x)$.

   a. x
   b. 2x
   c. x/2
   d. x/3

10. $\{a_n\} = \{2, 4, 6, ...\}$ and $\{b_n\} = \{4, 9, 14, ...\}$ are arithmetic sequences, each with 50 terms. How many common terms do these two sequences have?

   a. 4
   b. 6
   c. 8
   d. 10

11. What is the result of $(\log_x y / \log_{xz} y^3) - \log_x \sqrt[3]{z}$?

   a. 1/3
   b. 1/27
   c. 3
   d. 9

12. A ball 32 cm above the floor is attached to the end of a spring attached to the ceiling. Initially, we pull the ball 6 cm down and when we let it move, it performs one up and down motion in 4 seconds. Modeling this harmonic movement using trigonometric functions (Assume that there is no air friction), find the distance between the ball and the ceiling at t = 9.5 seconds. Round your answer to the nearest hundredths.

    a. 28.12 cm
    b. 30.28 cm
    c. 32.36 cm
    d. 36.24 cm

13. Which of the following functions have the largest domain?

	F(x)
I	$(x + 1) / 9x - 2$
II	$(x + 7) / (x^2 + 5x + 6)$
III	$(x^2 - 9) / (x + 3)$
IV	$(4x + 7) / (9x^2 - 4)$

    a. I
    b. II
    c. III
    d. IV

14. Find the range of the function $(2x + 3) / (x^2 - x + 2) < 0$.

    a. $(-\infty, -2) \cup (-2, +\infty)$
    b. $(-\infty, -3/2) \cup (-1, 2)$
    c. $\{-3/2, -1, 2\}$
    d. $(-\infty, -3/2) \cup (-1, +\infty)$

15. Describe the end behavior of the polynomial P(x) = (2x - 5)(3 - x)(4x² + 7).

   a. $y \to 0$ as $x \to -\infty$ and $y \to -\infty$ as $x \to \infty$
   b. $y \to -\infty$ as $x \to -\infty$ and $y \to \infty$ as $x \to \infty$
   c. $y \to -\infty$ as $x \to -\infty$ and $y \to -\infty$ as $x \to \infty$
   d. $y \to -\infty$ as $x \to -\infty$ and $y \to 0$ as $x \to \infty$

Part IV - Calculus

1. Find the difference between the integral of f(x) = 2x² and the area under this graph of this function using the Riemann sum with Δx = 1, within the interval [-3, 3].

   a. 12
   b. 15
   c. 18
   d. 20

2. Given $F(x) = \int_{1}^{x}(2t + 1)dt$, which of the following is the equation of the line that is tangent to F(x) at x = 2 ?

   a. y = 2x + 5
   b. y = 5x - 6
   c. y = 6x + 5
   d. y = 7x - 2

3. Using the definition of definite integral, compute $\int_0^4 x^2 dx$.

   a. 64/3
   b. 32
   c. 48
   d. 64

4. Given the graph of f'(x); which of the following graphs represent the plot of function f(x)?

a.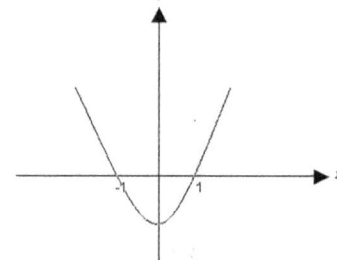

b.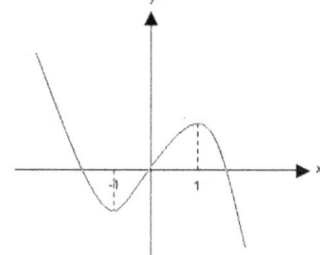

c.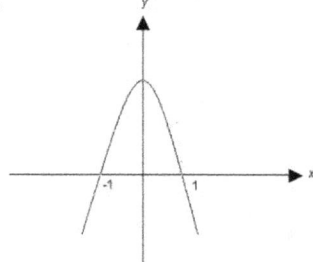

d.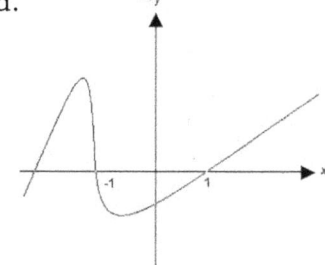

Practice Test Questions 2

5. Find the interval of convergence of the power series

$$\sum_{n=1}^{\infty} ((x - 1)^n / (2n + 1)).$$

    a. -1 < x < 1
    b. -1 < x < 2
    c. 0 < x < 2
    d. 1 < x < 3

6. Jane and Kevin are standing 5 m apart. Jane starts walking north with a constant velocity and so, θ changes at a constant rate of 50/min. Find the rate of distance in m/min between Jane and Kevin when θ = 35°. Round your answer to the nearest hundredths.

    a. 15.40 m/min
    b. 21.37 m/min
    c. 35.45 m/min
    d. 48.76 m/min

7. Given dy/dx = x^2y - 2y and y(0) = 1, find the value of integration constant.

    a. -1
    b. 0
    c. 2
    d. 4

8. Using the limit definition, compute the derivative of f(x) = cos5x.

    a. 5cos5x
    b. -5cos5x
    c. 5sin5x
    d. -5sin5x

9. Given $F(x) = \int_{\pi/4}^{x} \cos^2 t \, dt$, which of the following is the equation of the line that is tangent to $F(x)$ at $x = \pi/2$?

    a. $y = (\pi + 1) - x/4$
    b. $y = y = (\pi + 1) / 4 + x$
    c. $y = (\pi - 1) / 4$
    d. $y = x/4 - \pi/8$

10. **Find the inflection point of the function $-(1/6)x^3 - x^2$.**

    a. -4
    b. -2
    c. 0
    d. 2

Part V - Geometry and Measurement

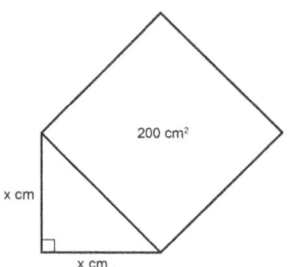

Note: Figure not drawn to scale

1. What is the length of the sides in the triangle above? Assume the quadrangle in the figure above is a square.

   a. 10
   b. 20
   c. 100
   d. 40

2. If in the right triangle, a is 12 and sinα=12/13, find cosα.

   a. -5/13
   b. -1/13
   c. 1/13
   d. 5/13

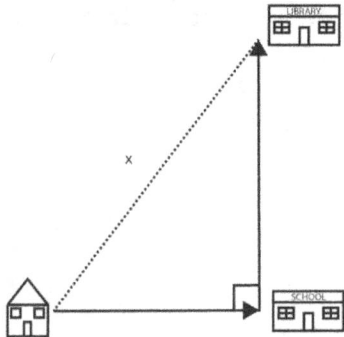

Note: Figure not drawn to scale

3. Every day starting from his home Peter travels due east 3 kilometers to the school. After school he travels due north 4 kilometers to the library. What is the distance between Peter's home and the library?

   a. 15 km
   b. 10 km
   c. 5 km
   d. 12 ½ km

4. Reflect the triangle ABC with the given mirror line m.

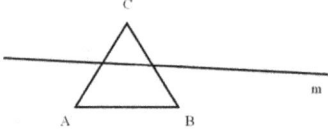

5. Reflect the rectangle ABCD with the given mirror line m.

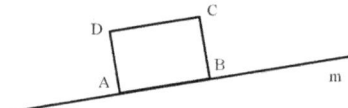

6. Reflect the quadrilateral ABCD in the coordinate plane if the mirror line is y-axis.

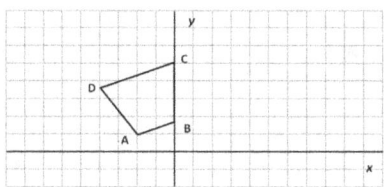

7. What are the respective correct values of a, b & c if both triangles are similar?

    a. 70°, 70°, 35°
    b. 70°, 35°, 70°
    c. 35°, 35°, 35°
    d. 70°, 75°, 35°

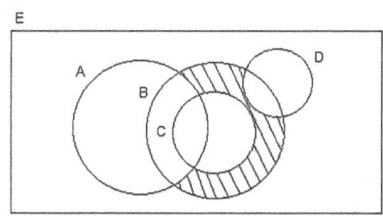

8. Which choice above represent the shaded region?
    a. B \ (A ∪ C ∪ D)
    b. A' ∩ D' ∩ C
    c. (D' ∩ B) ∩ (A ∪ C)
    d. (C' ∪ B') ∩ (A ∩ D')

9. The interior angles of a triangle are consecutive even numbers. If the middle angle is equal to one angle of a parallelogram, find the other angle of the parallelogram.

    a. 80°
    b. 94°
    c. 120°
    d. 135°

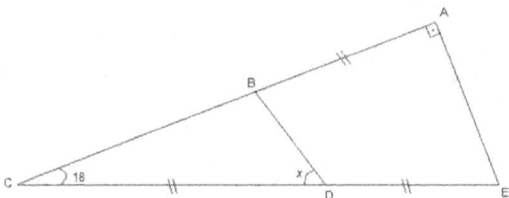

Note: figure not drawn to scale

10. ACE is a triangle with [CA] ⊥ [AE], |AB| = |DE| = |CD| and m ∠ BCD = 180. Find the value of x.

    a. $27°$

    b. $35°$

    c. $63°$

    d. $75°$

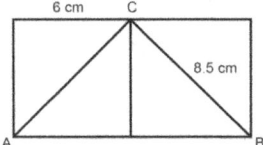

Note: figure not drawn to scale

11. Assuming the two quadrangles in the figure are identical rectangles, what is perimeter of △ABC in the above shape?

    a. 25.5 cm

    b. 27 cm

    c. 30 cm

    d. 29 cm

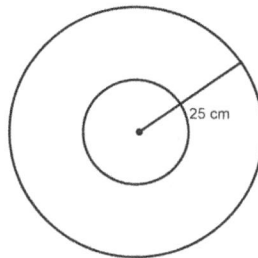

Note: figure not drawn to scale

12. What is the distance travelled by the wheel above, when it makes 175 revolutions?

    a. 87.5 π m

    b. 875 π m

    c. 8.75 π m

    d. 8750 π m

13. Find the center of the hyperbola represented by the equation $64y^2 - 25x^2 - 384y - 100x - 1124 = 0$.

    a. (-2, -3)

    b. (-2, 3)

    c. (3, -2)

    d. (3, 2)

14. Slope of line d_1 is the half of the slope of line d_2, and lines d_2 and d_3 are perpendicular. If the equation of line d_1 is given as $y = 2x + 5$, find the slope of line d_3.

    a. -1/4

    b. -1

    c. 1/4

    d. 4

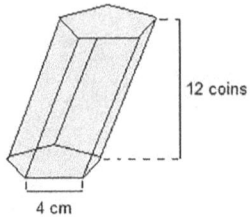

12 coins

4 cm

Note: Figure not drawn to scale

15. Here is an oblique shape of 12 coins put one over the other. The coins are regular pentagons with 1.2 cm thickness. What is the volume of the shape above? Round each step of calculation to the nearest hundredths.

    a. 288 cm^3

    b. 396 cm^3

    d. 425 cm^3

    d. 512 cm^3

Part VI - Statistics and Probability

1. There is a die and a coin. The dice is rolled and the coin is flipped according to the number the die is rolled. If the die is rolled only once, what is the probability of 4 successive heads?

    a. 3/64

    b. 1/16

    c. 3/16

    d. 1/4

2. These numbers are taken from the number of people that attended church every Friday for 7 weeks – 62, 18, 39, 13, 16, 37, 25. Find the mean.

    a. 25
    b. 210
    c. 62
    d. 30

3. F(x) function is defined by:

$$F(x) = \begin{cases} 0.2; & x > 0 \\ 0.5; & 0 \leq x < 5 \\ 0.8; & 5 \leq x < 10 \\ 1; & 10 \leq x \end{cases}$$

For the discontinuous random variable X, find P(4 < X < 15).

    a. 0.3
    b. 0.5
    c. 0.6
    d. 0.8

4. Smith and Simon are playing a card game. Smith will win if the drawn card form the deck of 52 is either 7 or a diamond, and Simon will win if the drawn card is an even number. Which statement is more likely to be correct?

    a. Smith will win more games.
    b. Simon will win more games.
    c. They have same winning probability.
    d. Decision could not be made from the provided data.

5. In a museum, there are 250 visitors. An interviewer asks 50 people the number of days they visit museums per year. Here is the data obtained:

# of days museum visited per year	# of visitors interviewed
5	12
3	18
12	8
20	2
4	10

Based on the data, what is the most reasonable estimate for the number of visitors who visit museums 20 days in a year?

    a. 2
    b. 8
    c. 10
    d. 12

6. Find the mode from these test results - 90, 80, 77, 86, 90, 91, 77, 66, 69, 65, 43, 65, 75, 43, 90

    a. 43
    b. 77
    c. 65
    d. 90

7. Sarah has two children and we know that she has a daughter. What is the probability that the other child is a girl as well?

    a. 1/4
    b. 1/3
    c. 1/2
    d. 1

8. In an exhibition area, there are 100 bulbs and 9 of them are damaged. 12 bulbs are chosen randomly. What is the probability to choose exactly 3 damaged bulbs? Round your answer to the nearest hundredths.

   a. 0.03
   b. 0.08
   c. 0.11
   d. 0.18

9. A box contains 30 red, green and blue balls. The probability of drawing a red ball is twice the other colors due to its size. The number of green balls are 3 more than twice the number of blue balls, and blue are 5 less than the twice the red. What is the probability that 1st two balls drawn from the box randomly will be red?

   a. 10/102
   b. 11/102
   c. 1/29
   d. 1/30

10. A die is rolled; let X be equal to 2 times the number seen on the die and let Y be 1 if the number is odd and 3 if the number is even. Find the expected value of X + Y.

    a. 5.0
    b. 6.2
    c. 8.4
    d. 9.0

Skills and Competencies

Number and Quantity

1. Perform operations with rational numbers

2. Rewrite expressions with radical and rational numbers

3. Perform operations with complex numbers

4. Perform operations on matrices

5. Solve compound interest word problems

6. Solve equations with rational or radical expressions

7. Solve problems involving velocity and quantities using vectors

8. Solve equations using order of operation

9. Estimate answers

10. Solve word problems

11. Solve acceleration problems

12. Solve acceleration problems

13. Solve problems involving force

14. Solve problems involving force

15. Solve quadratics equations using different methods

16. Solve quadratic equations using different methods

17. Factor quadratic equations

18. Factor quadratic equations

19. Solve velocity problems

20. Solve acceleration problems

Algebra

1. Perform operations with polynomials

2. Perform operations with polynomials

3. Graphs of functions

4. Solve real world problems with quadratics

5. Solve problems using graphs of quadratics

6. Perform operations with exponents

7. Perform operations with polynomials

8. Solve inequalities

9. Perform operations with quadratic equations

10. Solve real world proportion problems

11. Solve real world proportion problems

12. Solve linear equations with 1 variable

13. Solve linear equations with 1 variable

14. Solve linear equations with 1 variable

15. Perform operations with polynomials

16. Identify equation of line that is perpendicular or parallel to a given line

17. Analyze rates and proportional relationships and use them to solve real-world mathematical problems

18. Rewrite and manipulate rational expressions

19. Create equations and inequalities to describe a linear process

20. Represent and solve linear and nonlinear equations and inequalities graphically

Functions

1. Determine the domain of a function

2. Understand and calculate first derivatives

3. Understand and calculate antiderivatives

4. Understand and use sequences and recursive functions

5. Perform operations with functions

6. Perform operations with functions

7. Understand and calculate inverse functions

8. Understand and calculate inverse functions

9. Understand and calculate inverse functions

10. Understand and use arithmetic and geometric sequences

11. Solve logarithmic and exponential functions

12. Model periodic phenomena with trigonometric functions

13. Determine the domain and range of a given table of values

14. Determine the range of a function

15. Determine the end behavior of a function

Calculus

1. Interpret derivatives and definite integrals as limits (difference quotients, slope, Riemann sums area)

2. Use the fundamental theorem of calculus

3. Define and compute integrals

4. Apply properties of derivatives to analyze the graphs of functions.

5. Compute power Series

6. Use derivatives to solve rates of change, related rates, optimization.

7. First order differential equations - separation of variables, initial value problems

8. Compute the definition of limit

9. Use the fundamental theorem of Calculus

10. Apply properties of derivatives to analyze the graphs of functions

Geometry and Measurement

1. Apply the Pythagorean theorem to solve problems

2. Use right angle trigonometry

3. Apply the Pythagorean theorem to solve problems

4. Apply properties of reflection

5. Apply properties of reflection

6. Apply properties of reflection

7. Understand Similarity

8. Perform operations with open and closed sets

9. Perform calculations with lines, angles, triangles, parallelograms

10. Solve problems using right triangle trigonometry

11. Calculate perimeter

12. Calculate perimeter

13. Translate descriptions and equations of conic sections

14. Calculate the slope of perpendicular line

15. Calculate volume using Cavalieri's principle

Part VI - Statistics and Probability

1. Solve problems with dependent and independent variables

2. Calculate the mean of a data set

3. Solve problems with discontinuous random variables

4. Solve problems with simple probability

5. Make inferences about a population from a single random sample

6. Calculate the mode of a data set

7. Use Independence and conditional probability to interpret data

8. Independent and conditional probability

9. Solve problems using simple probability

10. Expected Value

Practice Test Questions 2 129

Answer Key

Part I - Number and Quantity

1. B
We need to find the difference between A and the expression given. Compare the fractions having the same denominator:

16/7 - 2/7 = 14/7 = 2

22/9 - 4/9 = 18/9 = 2

-5/11 - 6/11 = -11/11 = -1

Overall; the expression given is 2 + 2 - 1 = 4 more than A (A + 4).

2. B
In this question, notice that there are different degrees of roots. When no number is mentioned as degree, it is square root. There are also 3rd and 4th degree of roots in this question. When taking the nth root of a number, we need to consider in the opposite direction. The nth root of the number is the number of which nth power is the number inside the root. So, √(4/9) = √4/√9 = 2/3 since the square of 2 is 4 and the square of 3 is 9. Similarly; ³√125 = ³√5³ = 5 and ⁴√81 = ⁴√3⁴ = 3. Inserting these equivalences and doing the fractional operations, step by step solution is as follows:

(√(4/9) * 3/8) / ((³√125 / ⁴√81) / 4 - 1/12) = (2/3 * 3/8) / (5/3 * 1/4 - 1/12)
= (1/4) / (5/12 - 1/12)
= (1/4) / ((5 - 1) / 12) = (1/4) / (4/12) = 1/4 * 12/4 = 3/4

3. B
We know that i^2 = -1. However, in this question, we see high powers of i. We need to use modular arithmetic techniques to solve this problem:

i^0 = 1
i^1 = i
i^2 = -1

$i^3 = -i$
$i^4 = 1$
$i^5 = i$

This means that every 4 powers; we obtain i. So, by dividing the powers by 4; the remainder of the division operation will lead us to the result of powers:

$18/4 \rightarrow$ remainder = 2
$5/4 \rightarrow$ remainder = 1
$162/4 \rightarrow$ remainder = 2
$39/4 \rightarrow$ remainder = 3

Then;

$(i^{18} - i^5 + 4i^{162} - i^{39}) / (i^2 - 1) = (i^2 - i + 4 \cdot i^2 - i^3) / (-1 - 1)$

$= (-1 - i - 4 * 1 + i) / (-2)$

$= (-5) / (-2) = 5/2$

4. D
Notice that the dimensions for matrix A and B are 2 x 2 and 2 x 2, respectively. In matrix multiplication; the dimensions are important. Since A * X = B, the dimensions of matrix X should be 2 x 2. Let us say that matrix X is as follows:

$$X = \begin{bmatrix} a & b \\ c & d \end{bmatrix} \text{ So, } \begin{bmatrix} 1 & 4 \\ 1 & 3 \end{bmatrix} \begin{bmatrix} a & b \\ c & d \end{bmatrix} = \begin{bmatrix} 2 & 2 \\ 5 & 1 \end{bmatrix}$$

Now, let us write equations obtained from matrix multiplication:

1a + 4c = 2 ... (I)
1b + 4d = 2 ... (II)
1a + 3c = 5 ... (III)
1b + 3d = 1 ... (IV)

Now, we have 4 unknowns and 4 equations which means that we will be able to find the values of a, b, c and d. Using equations (I) and (III), we will find a and c; using equations (II) and (IV), we will find b and d:

$$1a + 4c = 2 \ldots \text{(I)}$$
$$- / \ 1a + 3c = 5 \ldots \text{(III)}$$
$$4c - 3c = 2 - 5$$
$$c = -3$$

Inserting this value into equation (I): $1a + 4(-3) = 2$
a - 12 = 2
a = 14

$$1b + 4d = 2 \ldots \text{(II)}$$
$$- / \ 1b + 3d = 1 \ldots \text{(IV)}$$
$$4d - 3d = 2 - 1$$
$$d = 1$$

Inserting this value into equation (II): $1b + 4(1) = 2$
b + 4 = 2
b = -2

So, Matrix $X = \begin{bmatrix} a & b \\ c & d \end{bmatrix}$ is:

$$X = \begin{bmatrix} 14 & -2 \\ -3 & 1 \end{bmatrix}$$

5. C
Insert the given values into the compound interest formula
$A = P * (1 + r/n)^{n \cdot t}$
where,

P: initial amount deposited in the bank
r: annual rate of interest (written in decimal form)
n: number of times the interest is compounded per year
t: number of years passing
A: amount of money accumulated in the bank, including the interest

Notice that 15% rate of interest is applied annually which means that n is 1 in this question. Mary invests $1,000 every year, so we need to write 5 terms and sum them up for

5 years:

A = 1,000 (1 + 0.15)^5 + 1,000 (1 + 0.15)^4 + 1,000 (1 + 0.15)^3 + 1,000 (1 + 0.15)^2 + 1,000 (1 + 0.15)^1

= 1,000 (1.15^5 + 1.15^4 + 1.15^3 + 1.15^2 + 1.15^1)

Here, we need to use the formula:

x^n + x^{n-1} + x^{n-2} + ... + x^1 = x * (x^n - 1) / (x - 1)

So,

A = 1,000 * (1.15) * (1.15^5 - 1) / (1.15 - 1)

≈ 7,753.74

When rounded to the nearest integer; Mary will have $7,754 after 5 years. Remember that she invests $1,000 initially and $1,000 every year. In total, she invests $5,000. Since her money in the bank is $7,754 after 5 years, we conclude that her profit is 7,754 - 5,000 = $2,754.

6. D

In this type of question with one root within the other, we need to reduce the expression to one root with one degree that is found by multiplying all degrees of roots that follow.

Meanwhile; while taking a number inside a root, we need to take its power that is the degree of the root:

$\sqrt[4]{2 * \sqrt[3]{4}} * \sqrt[3]{\sqrt{8}} = \sqrt[6]{4 * \sqrt[2]{2^{x+1}}}$

= $\sqrt[4.3]{2^3 * 4} * \sqrt[3.2]{8} = \sqrt[6.2]{4^2 * 2^{x+1}}$

Notice that every term is a power of 2, so let us write all of them in base 2:

= $\sqrt[12]{2^3 * 2^2} * \sqrt[6]{2^3} = \sqrt[12]{2^4 * 2^{x+1}}$

= $\sqrt[12]{2^5} * \sqrt[6]{2^3} = \sqrt[12]{2^{x+5}}$

= $2^{5/12} * 2^{3/6} = 2^{(x+5)/12}$

$= 2^{(5/12 + 1/2)} = 2^{(x+5)/12}$

Now that the bases are the same, we can equate the powers:

5/12 + 1/2 = (x + 5) / 12

(5 + 6) / 12 = (x + 5) / 12

11 = x + 5

x = 6

7. D
We need to write equations with the two data provided:
If they move towards each other, they meet in city B. Since the time information is the same for both vehicles, we can equate distance/velocity ratios. Let us name |AB| = a, |BC| = b and |CD| = c:

|AB| / 100 = |BC| / 80

a / 100 = b / 80 → a / 5 = b / 4 → 4a = 5b

If both vehicles move towards city D, they meet there. Again, time information is the same for both vehicles, so:

|CD| / 80 = |AD| / 100

c / 80 = (a + b + c) / 100 → c / 4 = (a + b + c) / 5 → 5c = 4a + 4b + 4c

→ 4a + 4b = c

We are asked to find |CD| / |BC| that is c / b:
We have:

4a = 5b ... (I)

4a + 4b = c ... (II)

Inserting equation (I) into equation (II):

5b + 4b = c

9b = c

So, c / b = 9b / b = 9

8. D
120 ÷ (6 + 12 x 2) = 4

9. B
46,227 + 101,032 = about 147,000. The actual amount is 147,259.

10. C
Total expense is $2000 and we are informed that $5 is spent per meter. Combining this information, we calculate the total length of the fence is 2000/5 = 400 meters.

The fence is built around a square-shaped field. If one side of the square is "a," the perimeter of the square is "4a." Here, the perimeter is equal to 400 meters. So,

400 = 4a

100 = a → this means that one side of the square is equal to 100 meters.

11. A
The formula for acceleration = A = $(V_f - V_0)/t$

so A = (120 - 90)/5 sec = 6 mph/second

12. C
Speed = (distance traveled)/(time)

1000/5 = 200 meters per second

13. C
Force = Mass times Acceleration Measured in Newtons.

F = 2000 kg X 3 m/sec² = 6000 N

14. B
Force = Mass times Acceleration (measured in Newtons)

F = 200 X 5 = 1000 N

15. A

$2x^2 - 3x = 0$ ... we see that both of the terms contain x; so we can take it out as a factor:

$x(2x - 3) = 0$ ... two terms are multiplied and the result is zero. This means that either of the terms or, both can be equal to zero:

$x = 0$ ... this is one solution

$2x - 3 = 0 \rightarrow 2x = 3 \rightarrow x = 3/2 \rightarrow x = 1.5$ ... this is the second solution.

So, the solutions are 0 and 1.5.

16. A

To solve the equation, we need the equation in the form $ax^2 + bx + c = 0$.

$x^2 - 9x + 14 = 0$ is already in this form.

The quadratic formula to find the roots of a quadratic equation is:

$x_{1,2} = (-b \pm \sqrt{\Delta}) / 2a$ where $\Delta = b^2 - 4ac$ and is called the discriminant of the quadratic equation.

In our question, the equation is $x^2 - 9x + 14 = 0$. By remembering the form $ax^2 + bx + c = 0$:

$a = 1, b = -9, c = 14$

So, we can find the discriminant first, and then the roots of the equation:

$\Delta = b^2 - 4ac = (-9)^2 - 4 * 1 * 14 = 81 - 56 = 25$

$x_{1,2} = (-b \pm \sqrt{\Delta}) / 2a = (-(-9) \pm \sqrt{25}) / 2 = (9 \pm 5) / 2$

This means that the roots are,

$x_1 = (9 - 5) / 2 = 2$ and $x_2 = (9 + 5) / 2 = 7$

17. D

$9x^2 - 6x + 12 = 3 * \underline{3x^2} - 2 * \underline{3x} + \underline{3} * 4 = 3(3x^2 - 2x + 4)$

18. A

$x^3y^3 - x^2y^8 = x \cdot \underline{x^2y^3} - \underline{x^2y^3} \cdot y^5 = x^2y^3(x - y^5)$

19. D

Speed = (total distance traveled)/(total time taken)

3000/5 = 600 meters per second.

20. D

The formula for acceleration = $A = (V_f - V_0)/t$

so A = (20 m/sec - 0 m/sec)/10 sec = 2 m/sec^2

Part II - Algebra

1. A

Write in standard form
$(3y^5 + y^4 + 2y^3 - 2y + 5) - (2y^5 + 3y^3 + 7y + 2)$

Arrange in columns of like terms and subtract bottom row

$$3y^5 + y^4 + 2y^3 - 2y + 5$$
$$-2y^5 - 3y^3 - 7y - 2$$
$$\overline{}$$
$$y^5 + y^4 - y^3 - 9y + 3$$

2. B

$(-3x^2 + 2x + 6) + (-x^2 - x - 1)$

$= -3x^2 + 2x + 6 - x^2 - x - 1$ ... we write similar terms together:

$= -3x^2 - x^2 + 2x - x + 6 - 1$ ... we operate within the same terms:

$= -4x^2 + x + 5$

3. C

First, we need to find the formula of the linear function. We are given that the line passes through points

(4, 0) and (0, 3). Since we know two points on a line, we can find the line formula by finding the slope (*m*) of the line first using:

$m = (y_2 - y_1) / (x_2 - x_1)$

Here, let us say that the 1st point is (4, 0) and the 2nd is (0, 3):

$m = (y_2 - y_1) / (x_2 - x_1) = (3 - 0) / (0 - 4) = -3/4$

Now, since we know the value of the slope, we can write the line equation by using the formula:

$y - y_1 = m(x - x_1)$

$y - 0 = (-3/4)(x - 4)$

$y = -3x/4 + 3$

Up to this step, we have found that f(x) = -3x/4 + 3. Now, we need to find the inverse of this function.

To find f⁻¹(x), we need to replace *x* and *y* and find the equation of *y*:

$x = -3y/4 + 3$

$x - 3 = -3y/4$

$y = (4/3)(3 - x)$

$y = 4 - 4x/3$

So, f⁻¹(x) = 4 - 4x/3. We are asked to find f⁻¹(2). Inserting x = 2:

$f^{-1}(2) = 4 - 4*2 / 3 = 4 - 8/3 = (12 - 8) / 3 = 4/3$

4. B
There are two statements which give two equations:

The sum of two numbers are 21: x + y = 21

The sum of the squares is 261: $x^2 + y^2 = 261$

We are asked to find x and y.

Since we have the sums of the numbers and the sums of

their squares; we can use the square formula of x + y, that is:

$(x + y)^2 = x^2 + 2xy + y^2$ ... Here, we can insert the known values x + y and $x^2 + y^2$:

$(21)^2 = 261 + 2xy$ ... Arranging to find xy:

441 = 261 + 2xy

441 - 261 = 2xy

180 = 2xy

xy = 180/2

xy = 90

We need to find two numbers which multiply to 90. Checking the answer choices, we see that in (b), 15 and 6 are given.

15 * 6 = 90. Also their squares sum up to 261 ($15^2 + 6^2$ = 225 + 36 = 261) and satisfy the equation.

5. D
The coordinates where f "(x) is zero give the vertexes of the function. Here, we observe that the second derivative of the function is equal to zero when x is -1, 2, 4 and 7.

Then the sum of these values is: -1 + 2 + 4 + 7 = 12.

6. A
10 x 10 x 100 x 100 = 1000^x, =100 x 10,000 = 1000^x, = 1,000,000 = 1000^x = x = 2

7. C
We are asked to find A + B - C. By paying attention to the sign distribution; we write the polynomials and operate:

A + B - C = $(-2x^4 + x^2 - 3x) + (x^4 - x^3 + 5) - (x^4 + 2x^3 + 4x + 5)$

= $-2x^4 + x^2 - 3x + x^4 - x^3 + 5 - x^4 - 2x^3 - 4x - 5$

= $-2x^4 + x^4 - x^4 - x^3 - 2x^3 + x^2 - 3x - 4x + 5 - 5$ ... similar terms written together to ease summing/substituting.

= $-2x^4 - 3x^3 + x^2 - 7x$

8. C

To find the solution for the inequality, we need to simplify it first:

$(x - 6)^2 \geq x^2 + 12$ ... we can write the open form of the left side:

$x^2 - 12x + 36 \geq x^2 + 12$ ... x^2 terms on both sides cancel each other:

$-12x + 36 \geq 12$ ... Now, we aim to have x alone on one side. So, we subtract 36 from both sides:

$-12x + 36 - 36 \geq 12 - 36$

$-12x \geq -24$ ... We divide both sides by -12. This means that the inequality will change its direction:

$x \leq 2$ ... x can be 2 or a smaller value.

This result is shown by $(-\infty, 2]$.

Note: The square parenthesis means that the limit on its side is included to the solution and in our solution, 2 is included.

9. A

We are asked to multiply $(x - 1)(x^2 + x + 2)$.

Each term in the first parenthesis $(x - 1)$ should be multiplied to each term in the second parenthesis $(x^2 + x + 2)$:

we write similar terms together:

$= x(x^2 + x + 2) - 1(x^2 + x + 2) = x^3 + x^2 + 2x - x^2 - x - 2$

we operate within the same terms

$= x^3 + x^2 - x^2 + 2x - x - 2$

x^2 and $-x^2$ cancel:

$= x^3 + x - 2$

10. B
The area of a rectangle is the width * height or, ab.

$ab = 20 \rightarrow a = 20/b$

$(a + 1)(b + 2) = 35$

$(20/b + 1)(b + 2) = 35$

$20 + 40/b + b + 2 = 35$

$20b + 40 + b^2 = 33b$

$b^2 - 13b + 40 = 0$

$b_{1,2} = (13 \pm \sqrt{169 - 160})/2$

$b_{1,2} = (13 \pm 3)/2$

$b_1 = 8$
$b_2 = 5$

$a_1 = 20/b_1 = 20/8 = 2.5$

$a_2 = 20/b_2 = 20/5 = 4$

11. B
$V_b = V_a - 20$
$S = 480$
$T_a + 2 = T_b$

$S = V_a T_a$
$T_a = S/V_a$
$T_a = S/V_a$

$480 = (V_a - 20)(T_a + 2)$

$480 = (V_a - 20)(480/V_a - 40)$

$480 = 480 + 2V_a - 20(480/V_a) - 40$

$2V2_a - 40V_a - 9600 = 0$

Practice Test Questions 2

$V_a^2 - 20V_a - 4800 = 0$

$V_{a1,2} = (20 \pm \sqrt{400 + * 4800})/2$

$V_{a1,2} = (20 \pm 140)/2$

$V_a = 80$

12. D
$5x/2 = (3x + 24)/6$

$3 * 5x/2 = (3x + 24)/6$

$15x/6 = (3x + 24)/6$

$15x = 3x + 24$

$15x - 3x = 24$

$12x = 24$

$x = 24/12 = 2$

13. A
$(a + 2)x - b = -2 + (a + b)x$

$ax + 2x - b = -2 + ax + bx$

$ax + 2x - ax - bx = -2 + b$

$2x - bx = -2 + b$

$(2 - b)x = -(2 - b)$

$x = -(2 - b):(2 - b)$

$x = -1$

14. D
$1/(4x - 2) = 5/6$

$1 = 5/6(4x - 2)$

$6 = 5(4x - 2)$

$6 = 20x - 10$

$-20x = -10 - 6$

$-20x = -16$

$x = -16/-20 = 0.08$

15. D
$(x^2 + x + 3)(2x^2 - 3x + 1) = ?$

$= x^2(2x^2 - 3x + 1) + x(2x^2 - 3x + 1) + 3(2x^2 - 3x + 1)$

$= x^2(2x^2) + x^2(-3x) + x^2(1) + x(2x^2) + x(-3x) + x(1) + 3(2x^2) + 3(-3x) + 3(1)$ (9 terms)

$= 2x^4 - 3x^3 + x^2 + 2x^3 - 3x^2 + x + 6x^2 - 9x + 3$

$= 2x^4 + (-3 + 2)x^3 + (1 - 3 + 6)x^2 + (1 - 9)x + 3$

$= 2x^4 - x^3 + 4x^2 - 8x + 3$

16. A
Line d_1, $y = ax + b$ that is parallel to $2y = 4x - 3$ must have the same slope with f. Function f can be written as $y = 2x - 3/2$ which makes it obvious that the slope is 2. Then, since the slope of d_1 is 2 as well; we conclude that $a = 2$: $y = 2x + b$.

If two lines d_1 and d_2 are perpendicular; the product of their slopes should be equal to -1:

$m_1 * m_2 = -1$. We know that $m_1 = 2$. So,

$2m_2 = -1$

$m_2 = -1/2$

So, equation of line d_2: $y = cx - b$ becomes $y = -x/2 - b$.

We know that $y = 2x + b$ and $y = -x/2 - b$ intersect at (2, d). Now, let us insert these coordinates into the equations of lines d_1 and d_2:

d = 2 * 2 + b

d = -2/2 - b

d = 4 + b

d = -1 - b

2d = 3

d = 3/2

17. A
The whole clock is 3600.
Every minute, the minute hand moves 360/60 = 6° and the hour hand moves 360/(60 * 12) = 0.5° = 1/2°

At 3:15, the minute hand shows directly "3" and the hour hand is 15 * 0.5 = 15/2° past it. We expect that the minute hand will get closer and pass the hour hand and then the angle between them will get larger. We are asked to find the time when the angle within the hands is 64°. We just need to set a simple equation and solve for x that is the minimum-number of minutes elapsing:

After x minutes, the minute hand will move 6x angles; the hour hand will move x/2 angles. The minute hand will move 15/20 initially that is the angle between the hands at 3:15; then it will pass the hour hand by 64°. So,

6x = 15/2 + x/2 + 64
(11/2)x = 15/2 + 128/2
(11/2)x = 143/2
11x = 143 → x = 13

After 13 minutes; at 3:28, the angle between hour and minute hands be 64°.

18. C
1 - 1/2 = 1/2
1 - 1/3 = 2/3

$1 - 1/4 = 3/4$

. .
. .
. .

$1 - 1/(x + 5) = (x + 5 - 1) / (x + 5) = (x + 4) / (x + 5)$

$(1 - 1/2) * (1 - 1/3) * (1 - 1/4) * \ldots * (1 - 1 / (x + 5)) = 1/18$

$1/2 * 2/3 * 3/4 \ldots (x + 4) / (x + 5) = 1/18$

Notice that starting from the first fraction; the denominator is cancelled by the numerator of the following fraction. After simplification, we have the following equation left:

$1 / (x + 5) = 1/18$

$x + 5 = 18$

$x = 13$

19. B

We are given that the bacteria reproduces exponentially; depending on time. So, we can write the growth function as:
$A = A_0 * e^{\gamma t}$

where A is the number of bacteria at any time

A_0 is the initial number of bacteria; that is $4 * 10^4$ in this question

t is time in hours

γ is the growth constant in hours^{-1}

We know that at t = 120 hours, $A = 1.024 * 10^{15}$ bacteria. Then,

$1.024 * 10^{15} = 4 * 10^4 * e^{\gamma \cdot 120}$

$2^{10} * 10^{12} = 2^2 * 10^4 * e^{120\gamma}$

$2^8 * 10^8 = e^{120\gamma}$

$20^8 = e^{120\gamma}$

$\ln 20^8 = \ln e^{120y}$

$8 * \ln 20 = 120y$

$y = \ln 20 / 15$

$y = 0.1997...$ when rounded to the nearest tenths: ≈ 0.2

20. C
Let us start analyzing the graph:

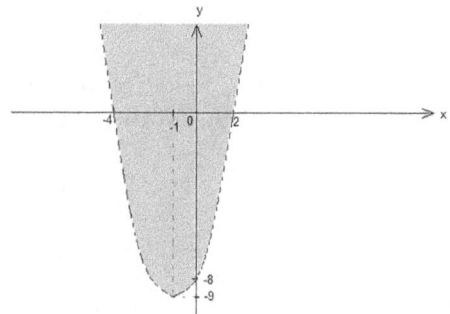

Step 1: It shows quadratic characteristics, the roots of the function are $x = -4$ and $x = 2$. Choices B and D can be eliminated since they are linear functions.

Step 2: The graph is concave up which means that the term x^2 has positive coefficient. The vertex passes through (-1, -9). The inequality does not cover 0 since the line is dashed.

Point (0, 0) is not included in the inequality. By inserting $x = 0$ and $y = 0$, we can check choices A and C:

$x^2 + 2x - 8 > 0$

$0^2 + 2 * 0 - 8 > 0$

$-8 > 0$ ... this is not a correct statement, so this is not the correct inequality.

$x^2 + 2x - 8 < 0$

$0^2 + 2 * 0 - 8 < 0$

-8 < 0 ... this is a correct statement. Yet, it is better that we check the other steps:

Step 1:

Find the roots of $x^2 + 2x - 8 = 0$:

$x^2 + 2x - 8 = (x + 4)(x - 2) = 0$

$x = -4$ and $x = 2$. So, step 1 is proven.

Step 2:

$x^2 + 2x - 8 < 0$ ... the coefficient of term x^2 is 1, so the arms of the graph is concave up. The vertex (-1, -9) should satisfy $x^2 + 2x - 8 = 0$:

$(-1)2 + 2(-1) - 8 = -9$

$1 - 2 - 8 = -9$

$-9 = -9$ ... The vertex is correct.

The inequality does not cover 0 since the line is dashed: $x^2 + 2x - 8 < 0$. Step 2 is proven.

Part III - Functions

1. C

If the function is $f(x) = x$; this will be definable for every x. However, there are some cases where we need to eliminate some ranges of x. In this question, there is a square root operation and a denominator.

The expression inside the square root cannot be negative. So:

$x + 7 \geq 0$

$x \geq -7$

On the other hand; the denominator cannot be zero since number divided by zero is not definable:

$x - 3 \neq 0$

$x \neq 3$

We have two limitations; x can neither be smaller than -7 nor equal to 3. So, the domain for this function is:

$[-7, +\infty) - \{3\}$ or we can also show by: $[-7, 3) \cup (3, +\infty)$.

2. A
To derive a function which is a fraction and both numerator and denominator depend on x, we use the following general formula:

$f(x) = g(x) / h(x) \rightarrow f'(x) = df/dx = (dg/dx * h - dh/dx * g) / h^2$

So,

$(d/dx) ((x^3 + 1) / (x - 2)) = [((d/dx) (x^3 + 1)) * (x - 2) - ((d/dx) (x - 2)) * (x^3 + 1)] / (x - 2)^2$

$= (3x^2(x - 2) - 1(x^3 + 1)) / (x - 2)^2$

$= (3x^3 - 6x^2 - x^3 - 1) / (x^2 - 4x + 4)$

$= (2x^3 - 6x^2 - 1) / (x^2 - 4x + 4)$

We are asked to do the polynomial division operation above and find the remainder:

$\quad 2x^3 - 6x^2 - 1 \quad | \quad \underline{x^2 - 4x + 4}$
$\underline{- / 2x^3 - 8x^2 + 8x} \quad \quad 2x + 2$
$\quad \quad 2x^2 - 8x - 1$
$\underline{- / 2x^2 - 8x + 8}$

-9 that is the remainder

3. D
There are two ways to check the statements: We can take the derivative of the antiderivatives to find out if we obtain the functions given or not. Or, we can integrate the given functions to check if we obtain the given antiderivatives or not. Let us choose the first option:

1. f(x) = x sin3x

We will perform $\int x \sin 3x \, dx$. Here, we need to apply the rule: $\int u \, dv = uv - \int v \, du$:

$u = x \rightarrow$ by integration: $du = dx$

$dv = \sin 3x \, dx \rightarrow$ by integration: $v = (-1/3) \cos 3x$

$\int x \sin 3x \, dx = x \, (-1/3) \cos 3x - \int (-1/3) \cos 3x \, dx$

$= (-1/3) \, x \cos 3x + (1/9) \sin 3x + C$

$= (-1/3) \, [x \cos 3x - (1/3) \sin 3x] + C$

There is a minus mistake in the answer, so the antiderivative given for 1 is wrong.

2. f(x) = 1 / (2√(3x³))

We will perform $\int dx / (2\sqrt{(3x^3)})$. After some organization:

$\int dx / (2\sqrt{(3x^3)}) = (1 / 2\sqrt{3}) \int x^{-3/2} \, dx = (\, (1 / 2\sqrt{3}) * (x^{-3/2+1}) / (-3/2 + 1) \,) + C$

$= (\, (1 / 2\sqrt{3}) * (x^{-1/2}) / (-1/2) \,) + C$

$= -1 / \sqrt{(3x)} + C$

This is the same result as the antiderivative given in the question; that is correct.

4. A
Let us start by writing some values of the function:

$x = 1 : f(1) = 3$

$x = 2 : f(2) = 2 * f(1)$

$x = 3 : f(3) = 3 * f(2) = 3 * 2 * f(1)$

$x = 4 : f(4) = 4 * f(3) = 4 * 3 * 2 * f(1)$

$x = 5 : f(5) = 5 * f(4) = 5 * 4 * 3 * 2 * f(1)$

Notice that the expansion of f(n) contains n! times f(1). So,

f(n) = n! * f(1)

f(n) = 3 * n!

is the general formula of the function. Then,

f(20) = 3 * 20!

5. B
f(x) = 2x + 5

g(x) = 5x + 2.

g∘f = g(f(x)) = g(2x + 5) = 5(2x + 5) + 2 = 10x + 25 + 2 = 10x + 27

6. D
f(x) = 1 + x^2

f∘f = f(f(x)) = f(1 + x^2) = 1 + (1 + x^2)^2 = 1 + 1 + 2x^2 + x^4 = 2 + 2x^2 + x^4

7. B
f(x) = 1 - x

f^{-1}(1 - x) = x

1 - x = t

x = 1 - t

f^{-1}(t) = 1 - t

f^{-1}(x) = 1 - x

f^{-1}(1/2) = 1 - 1/2 = 1/2

8. A
f(x) = 5x

g(x) = 7 - 2x

$f(x) - g(x) = 5x - (7 - 2x) = 5x - 7 + 2x = 7x - 7$

$(f(x) - g(x))^{-1}(f(x) - g(x)) = x$

$(f(x) - g(x))^{-1}(7x - 7) = x$

$7x - 7 = t$

$7x = t + 7$

$x = (t + 7)/7$

$(f(t) - g(t))^{-1}(t) = (t + 7)/7$

$(f(x) - g(x))^{-1}(x) = (x + 7)/7$

$(f(x) - g(x))^{-1}(0) = (0 + 7)/7 = 1$

9. C

$f^{-1}(f(x)) = x$

Treat f(x) as a variable, so instead of 2x we have 2f(x).

$2f(x) = x$

$f(x) = x/2$

10. D

First, write the general formulas for the terms of each sequence.

Sequence a_n starts with 2, and following terms are always 2 plus the previous. We can conclude:

$a_{k+1} = 2 + 2k$

Similarly, sequence b_n starts with 4 and following terms are always 5 plus the previous. Then write:

$b_{m+1} = 4 + 5m$

Common terms will be where, $2 + 2k = 4 + 5m$:

$2 + 2k = 4 + 5m$

$2k = 4 + 5m - 2$

$2k = 5m + 2$

$k = 5m/2 + 1$

Now, the question is: How many integer m values are there that result in integer k values in this equation?

We know that there are 50 terms in each sequence. So, the maximum value for both $k + 1$ and $m + 1$ is 50. Notice that m is divided by 2. Since the addition part 1 is an integer itself, we need to focus on the term $5m/2$. m values should be even numbers; let us say $m = 2a$, a is an integer. Also, we have the limitation that k can be 49 the most:

$49 \geq (5 * 2a / 2 + 1$

$48 \geq 5a$

$48/5 \geq a$

$9.6 \geq a$

So, a is maximum 9. This means that 10 integers can be assigned to a, which are integers from 0 to 9. So, 10 integers can be assigned to m that are 2 times integers from 0 to 9 (0, 2, 4, ... , 18). As a result; there are 10 possible cases when $2 + 2k = 4 + 5m$, meaning that there are 10 terms common in sequences $\{a_n\}$ and $\{b_n\}$.

11. A
This is a logarithm question which requires the application of many identities. First, notice that we can apply $\log a^b = b \log a$ in the denominator:

$(\log_x y / \log_{xz} y^3) - \log_x {}^3\sqrt{z} = (\log_x y / 3\log_{xz} y) - \log_x {}^3\sqrt{z}$

Then, we need to apply base change $\log_a b = \log_c b / \log_c a$ in the denominator to make the numerator and the denominator similar, and prepare a form to have the possibility of simplification:

$= (\log_x y / (3\log_x y / \log_x xz)) - \log_x {}^3\sqrt{z}$

Now, by simplification:

= $(\log_x xz) / 3 - \log_x \sqrt[3]{z}$

Now, organise the second term:

= $(\log_x xz) / 3 - \log_x z^{1/3}$

= $(\log_x xz) / 3 - \log_x z / 3$

Remember that $\log(a*b) = \log a + \log b$:

= $(\log_x x + \log_x z - \log_x z) / 3$

= $\log_x x / 3$

We know that $\log_a a = 1$:

= $1/3$

12. D

Talking about periodic functions, we need to determine the period and the amplitude first. Then, we need to decide the type of the trigonometric function to be used. Here, we know that at time t = 0, the spring is stretched 6 cm; so the ball is 32 - 6 = 26 cm above the floor, and at t = 4 seconds, it is again 26 cm above the floor and is ready to go up again. Period is the duration between two cases when the movement is in the same direction passing through the same point. So, period T = 4 seconds.

Now, we need to decide which trigonometric function to use. We know that the graph of sine is in the middle at t = 0. However, in this question; we have 26 cm at t = 0; that is the y-intercept. That is why, we use cosine.

We know that the period of cost is 2π. The general form of cosine in harmonic motion is coswt where

w = $2\pi/t$. Then, the cosine with period 4 is found by:

w = $2\pi/4 = \pi/2$

$\cos((\pi/2)t)$

The amplitude is the magnitude difference from the center of oscillation to negative and positive peaks; that is 6 cm and the center passes through 32 cm:

H(t) = 32 - 6 cos((π/2)t)

at t = 9.5 seconds;

H(9.5) = 32 - 6 cos((π/2) 9.5) = 32 - 6 cos (4π + 15π/20)

= 32 - 6 cos 3π/4 = 32 - 6 (-cosπ/4)

= 32 + 6$\sqrt{2}$ / 2

= 36.24 cm

13. C
Without any restrictions, the domain of a function is (-∞, +∞). The restrictions are found by checking the denominator of the function. If there are any values that make the denominator zero; since division by zero is undefined, these x values should be eliminated from the domain:
f(x) = (x + 1) / (x - 2) : Notice that the denominator is x - 2 and x = 2 value makes it zero, so makes the function is undefined. The domain of this function is (-∞, +∞) - {2}.

f(x) = (x + 7) / (x^2 + 5x + 6) : Notice that the denominator is x^2 + 5x + 6 which can be factored as

(x + 2)(x + 3).

Then, x = -2 and x = -3 values make the denominator zero, so the function is undefined. The domain of this function is (-∞, +∞) - {-3, -2}.

f(x) = (x^2 - 9) / (x + 3) : Notice that first, it is possible to simplify the function:

f(x) = (x^2 - 9) / (x + 3) = (x + 3)(x - 3) / (x + 3) = x - 3.

Then, the denominator has vanished; the domain of this function is (-∞, +∞).

f(x) = (4x + 7) / (9x^2 - 4) : Notice that the denominator is

$9x^2 - 4$ which can be factored as $(3x - 2)(3x + 2)$. It is not possible to simplify. Then, $x = 2/3$ and $x = -2/3$ values make the denominator zero, so make the function undefined. The domain of this function is $(-\infty, +\infty) - \{-2/3, 2/3\}$.

Function $(x^2 - 9) / (x + 3)$ has the largest domain.

14. B

There are two points important in this question:

> 1. The function is smaller than 0, which limits the range.

> 2. There are x values that make the denominator zero which make the function undefined. So, these values should be eliminated.

Let us analyze the function:

$(2x + 3) / (x^2 - x + 2) = (2x + 3) / ((x - 2)(x + 1))$

Now, we need to prepare the sign table to find the range where the function is smaller than 0. First, the roots are found:

$2x + 3 = 0 \rightarrow x = -3/2$

$x - 2 = 0 \rightarrow x = 2$

$x + 1 = 0 \rightarrow x = -1$

x	$-\infty$	-3/2	-1	2	$+\infty$
2x + 3		-	+	+	+
x + 1		-	-	+	+
x - 2		-	-	-	+
(2x + 3)/((x - 2(x + 1))		-	+	-	+

We are asked the range where $(2x + 3) / ((x - 2)(x + 1)) < 0$. The inequality is satisfied at $(-\infty, -3/2) \cup (-1, 2)$.

Notice that -3/2 is not included because the function is not equal to zero and -1 and 2 are not included since they make the denominator zero.

15. C
The degree of the polynomial and the sign of the leading term determine the end behavior of a polynomial. We do not need to expand the polynomial; by multiplying the x values in three parenthesis, clearly the leading term is $-8x^4$. Then, the degree of the polynomial is 4 and the leading term is negative. This means that its graph is downwards with end points → -∞. Even degree means that both left and right end points have the same characteristics; y → -∞ both as x → -∞ and x → ∞.

Part IV - Calculus

1. D
First, find the integral of the function within the interval given:

$$\int_{-3}^{3} 2x^2 dx = 2(x^3/3) \Big|_{-3}^{3} = (2/3)(27 - (-27)) = 36$$

Now, let us draw the rectangles to be used in Riemann sum.

The formula for this method is: $\sum_{i=0}^{n-1} f(x_i)\Delta x$.

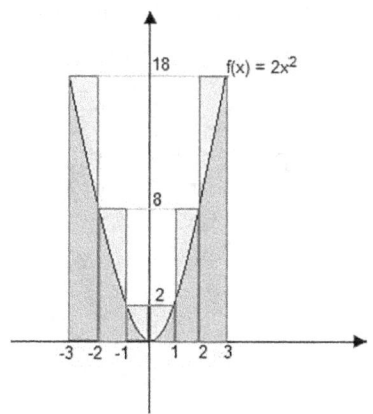

The smaller Δx value we use, the cleaner the calculation will be and the result will be closer to the integration result. In Riemann sum here, it is practical to find the total area between [0, 3] and multiply it by 2:

$$\sum_{i=0}^{n-1} f(x_i)\Delta x = 2[(1 - 0) * 2(1)^2 + (2 - 1) * 2(2)^2 + (3 - 2) * 2(3)^2]$$

$$= 2[1 * 2 + 1 * 8 + 1 * 18] = 2 * 28 = 56$$

The difference of Riemann sum - integration is: 56 - 36 = 20

2. B

The fundamental theorem of calculus mentions that, with f continuous on [a, b]:

1) If $F(x) = \int_{a}^{x} f(t)dt \rightarrow F'(x) = f(x)$

2) $\int_{a}^{b} f(t)dt = F(b) - F(a)$. where, F is the antiderivative of f.

We need information at x = 2. Solve step-by-step:

1) If $F(2) = \int_{1}^{2}(2t + 1)dt = (2t^2/2 + t)\Big|_{1}^{2} = (2^2 - 1^2) + (2 - 1) = 4$

$F'(2) = f(2) \rightarrow F'(2) = 2 * 2 + 1 = 5$

The line that is tangent to F(x) at x = 2 passes through (2, 4) with slope 5. Let us find the equation of this line using the formula:

$y - y_1 = m(x - x_1)$

$y - 4 = 5(x - 2)$

$y = 5x - 6$

3. A

Let us determine the interval of integration first. Accepting that there are n slices to be sum:

$\Delta x = (b - a.) / n = (4 - 0) / 4 = 4/n$

The subintervals are: $[0, 4/n], [4/n, 8/n], [8/n, 12/n], ..., [4(i - 1)/n, 4i/n], ..., [4(n - 1)/n, 4]$

Notice that the right endpoint of the ith subinterval is:

$x_i^0 = 4i/n$

The integral is the sum of the function over the subinterval pieces:

$$\sum_{i=1}^{n} f(x_i^0)\Delta x = \sum_{i=1}^{n} [f(4i/n)] * (4/n) = \sum_{i=1}^{n} (4i/n)^2 * (4/n)$$

$$= \sum_{i=1}^{n} 64i^2 / n^3 = 64/n^3 \sum_{i=1}^{n} i^2$$

Remember the sum:

$$\sum_{i=1}^{n} i^2 = n(n + 1)(2n + 1) / 6$$

$$\sum_{i=1}^{n} f(x_i^0)\Delta x = (64/n^3) * n(n + 1)(2n + 1) / 6 = (64/6) *$$

$((n + 1)(2n + 1)) / n^2$

To find the value of definite integral, we need to take the limit of the above expression:

$(64/6) \lim_{n \to \infty} (((n + 1)(2n + 1)) / n^2) = (64/6) \lim_{n \to \infty} ((2n^2 + 3n + 1)$

$/ n^2) = (64/6) \lim_{n \to \infty} ((n^2(2 + 3/n + 1/n^2) / n^2))$

$= (64/6) * (2 + 0 + 0) = 64/3$

4. B

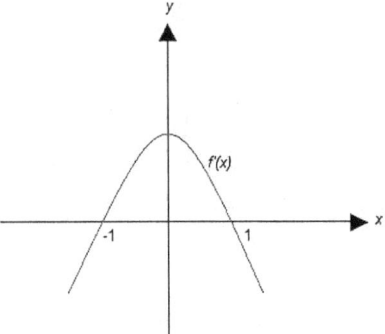

Checking the graph (above) of f'(x); we see that f' is negative when x < -1 and x > 1. This means that f is decreasing in this regions.

It is zero at x = -1 and x = 1 which mean that f has horizontal tangents at these points.

It is positive between (-1, 1). This means that f is increasing in this region.

Following these three notes, we see that the graph is as shown in choice B shown below.

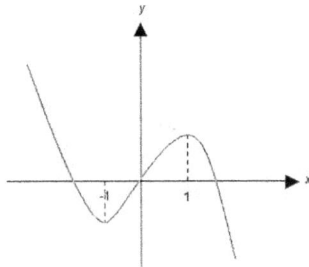

5. C

$\rho = \lim_{n \to \infty} |((x-1)^{n+1} / (2(n+1)+1)) / ((x-1)^n / (2n+1))|$

$= \lim_{n \to \infty} |(((x-1)^n \cdot (x-1)) / (2n+3)) / ((x-1)^n / (2n+1))|$

$= \lim_{n \to \infty} |((x-1)/(2n+3)) / (1/(2n+1))|$

= |x -1| * lim ((2n + 1) / (2n + 3))
       n→∞

= |x -1| * lim ((n(2 + 1/n)) / (n(2 + 3/n))) = |x -1|
       n→∞

-1 < x -1 < 1

0 < x < 2

The interval of convergence is 0 < x < 2.

6. B

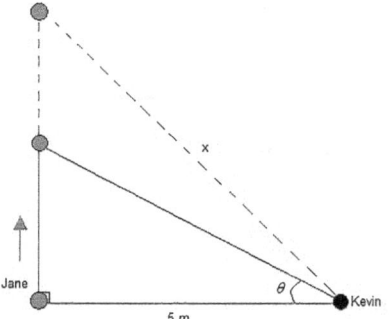

In the figure above, x is the distance between Jane and Kevin; we are asked to find the rate of change in x; that is x' when θ = 35^0.

Notice that both x and θ are time dependent: x(t) and θ(t).

Using right triangle properties:
cos θ = 5/x → x = 5/cos θ

Now, derive both sides:

(d/dt)x = d/dt 5/cos θ

x' = 5 sinθ * θ/$\cos^2$ θ

We are given that the rate of change of the angle is 5^0/min: θ' = 5^0/min and θ = 35^0. Inserting these values:

x' = 5sin35 * 5/$\cos^2$ 35 = 21.37m/min.

7. B
Noticing that the given differential equation is not ready to be integrated; we need to re-organise it by separation of variables:

$dy/dx = x^2y - 2y$

$dy/dx = y(x^2 - 2)$

$dy = y(x^2 - 2)dx$

$dy/y = (x^2 - 2)dx$ ... This form can be integrated:

$\int dy/y = \int (x^2 - 2)dx$

$\ln|y| = x^3/3 - 2x + C$

$|y| = e^{x^3/3 - 2x + C}$

Applying the initial value $y(0) = 1$ leads us to C:

$|y(0)| = e^{0 - 2.0 + C} = 1 \rightarrow e^C = 1 \rightarrow C = 0$

8. D
The derivative of a function as limit is found by:
$f'(x) = \lim_{\Delta x \to 0} (f(x + \Delta x) - f(x)) / \Delta x$

Here, $f(x) = \cos 5x$

$\rightarrow f(x + \Delta x) = \cos(5(x + \Delta x)) = \cos(5x + 5\Delta x)$

$f'(x) = \lim_{\Delta x \to 0} (f(x + \Delta x) - f(x)) / \Delta x = \lim_{\Delta x \to 0} (\cos(5x + 5\Delta x) - \cos 5x) / \Delta x$

Using the property: $\cos(a + b) = \cos a * \cos b - \sin a * \sin b$:

$= \lim_{\Delta x \to 0} (\cos 5x * \cos 5\Delta x - \sin 5x * \sin 5\Delta x - \cos 5x) / \Delta x$

$= \lim_{\Delta x \to 0} (\cos 5x(\cos 5\Delta x - 1) - \sin 5x * \sin 5\Delta x) / \Delta x$ ...

Recall that $\lim_{u \to 0} [(\cos u - 1) / u] = 0$ and $\lim_{u \to 0} (\sin u / u) = 1$

$= \lim_{\Delta x \to 0} [(\cos 5x(\cos 5\Delta x - 1)) / \Delta x] - \lim_{\Delta x \to 0} [(\sin 5x * \sin 5\Delta x) / \Delta x]$

$$= \lim_{\Delta x \to 0} [(5\cos5x(\cos5\Delta x - 1)) / 5\Delta x] - \lim_{\Delta x \to 0} [(5\sin5x * \sin5\Delta x) / 5\Delta x]$$

$$= 5\cos5x * \lim_{\Delta x \to 0} ((\cos5\Delta x - 1) / 5\Delta x) - 5\sin5x * \lim_{\Delta x \to 0} ((\sin5\Delta x) / 5\Delta x)$$

$$= 5\cos x * 0 - 5\sin5x * 1$$

$$= 0 - 5\sin5x$$

$$= -5\sin5x$$

9. C

The fundamental theorem of calculus mentions that, with f continuous on [a, b]:

1) If $F(x) = \int_a^x f(t)dt \rightarrow F'(x) = f(x)$

2) $\int_a^b f(t)dt = F(b) - F(a)$ where, F is the antiderivative of f.

We need information at $x = \pi/2$. Solve step-by-step:

1) If $F(\pi/2) = \int_{\pi/4}^{\pi/2} \cos^2 t \, dt = (t/2 + \sin2t / 4) \Big|_{\pi/4}^{\pi/2}$

$$= (1/2) * ((\pi/2) - (\pi/4)) + (1/4) * (\sin(2 * \pi/2) - \sin(2 * \pi/4))$$

$$= \pi/4 - 1/4 = (\pi - 1) / 4$$

$F'(\pi/2) = f(\pi/2) \rightarrow F'(\pi/2) = \cos^2(\pi/2) = 0$

The line that is tangent to F(x) at $x = \pi/2$ passes through $(\pi/2, (\pi - 1) / 4)$ with slope 0. Let us find the equation of this line using the formula:

$y - y_1 = m(x - x_1)$

$y - (\pi - 1) / 4 = 0(x - \pi/2)$

$y = (\pi - 1) / 4$

10. D

First, find the first derivative of the function:
$f(x) = -(1/6)x^3 - x^2$

$f'(x) = -(1/2)x^2 - 2x$ ... Now, find the x values where f' is zero:

$f'(x) = x((-1/2)x - 2) = 0$

$x = 0$ and $x = -4$

x:		-4		0	
sign of f':	−	|	+	|	−
behaviour of the graph:	↓	|	↑	|	↓

Now, find the second derivative:
$f''(x) = -x - 2$ ... Now, find the x values where f'' is zero:

$f''(x) = -x - 2 = 0$

$x = -2$

x:		−2	
sign of f'':	+	|	−
concavity of the graph:	up	|	down

Combine both charts to determine the graph behavior:

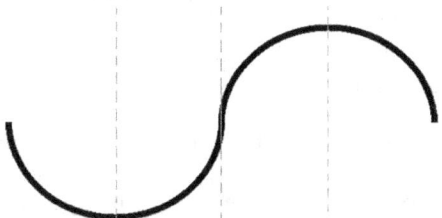

Notice that at x = 2, the graph changes its concavity; Meaning that, this is the inflection point.

Part V - Geometry and Measurement

1. A
If we call one side of the square "a," the area of the square will be a^2.

We know that $a^2 = 200$ cm².

On the other hand; there is an isosceles right triangle. Using the Pythagorean Theorem:

(Hypotenuse)² = (Adjacent Side)² + (Opposite Side)² Where the hypotenuse is equal to one side of the square. So,

$a^2 = x^2 + x^2$

$200 = 2x^2$

$200/2 = 2x^2/2$

$100 = x^2$

$x = \sqrt{100}$

$x = 10$ cm

2. D

To understand this question better, let us draw a right triangle by writing the given data on it:

Note: Figure not drawn to scale

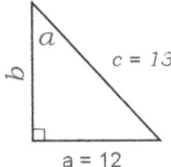

The side opposite angle a is named by a.

sin a = length of the opposite side / length of the hypotenuse = 12/13 is given.

cos a = length of the adjacent side / length of the hypotenuse = b/13

We use the Pythagorean Theorem to find the value of b:

(Hypotenuse)^2 = (Opposite Side)^2 + (Adjacent Side)^2

$c^2 = a^2 + b^2$

$13^2 = 12^2 + b^2$

$169 = 144 + b^2$

$b^2 = 169 - 144$

$b^2 = 25$

$b = 5$

So,

cos a = b/13 = 5/13

3. C

We see that two legs of a right triangle form by Peter's movements and we are asked to find the length of the hypotenuse. We use the Pythagorean Theorem:

(Hypotenuse)^2 = (Adjacent side)^2 + (Opposite side)^2

$h^2 = a^2 + b^2$

We know that a and b are 3 km and 4 km. So,

$h^2 = 3^2 + 4^2$

$h^2 = 9 + 16$

$h^2 = 25$

$h = \sqrt{25}$

$h = 5$ km

4.
We reflect points A, B and C against the mirror line m at the right angle and we connect the new points A', B' and C'. The process is the same even though the points of the triangle are not on the same side of the mirror line.

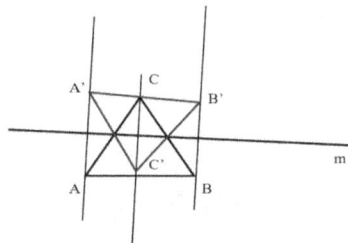

5.
We reflect points C and D against the mirror line m at the right angle. Since points A and B are already on the mirror line, we can't reflect them and that's why A coincides with point A', and the same goes for points B and B'.

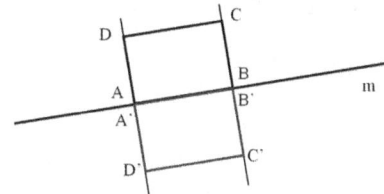

6.
The Apply properties of reflection process is the same in the coordinate plane. Here, our mirror line is y-axis, so we reflect points A and D, and points B and C are already on the mirror line, so we don't reflect them.

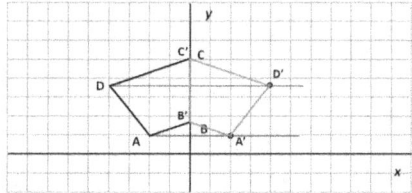

7. D

Comparing respective angles - 70°, 75°, 35°

8. A

The '\' sign in X\Y means the difference of the set X compared to set Y. In answer choice A, B \ (A ∪ C ∪ D) means B compared to union of A, C and D.

Set A ∪ C ∪ D is shown as below:

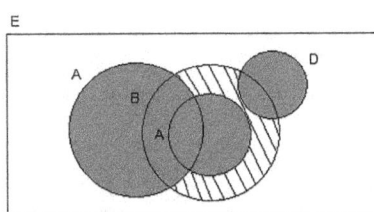

The difference of B compared to the red region is the shaded region.

Since we have found the correct choice, we do not have to try the other ones.

9. C

First, let us find the angles of the triangle. Let us name the smallest angle as a. Consequently; the middle angle is a + 2 and the larger one is a + 4. The sum of the three interior angles of a triangle is 1800. Then;

a + (a + 2) + (a + 4) = 180

3a = 174

a = 58^0

The middle angle is 58 + 2 = 60^0.

A parallelogram has four interior angles of which crosswise angles are equal. The sum of interior angles is 360^0. Then, the adjacent angle to 60^0 is supplementary to 60^0:

That is, 180 - 60 = 120^0

10. C

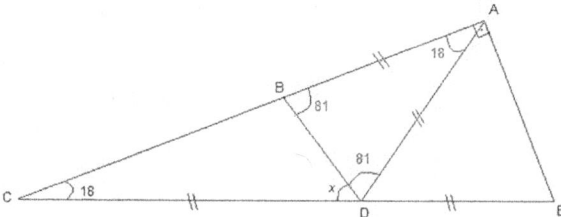

Note that in triangle ABD, since angles ABD and BDA are equal, their measure is found by:

m ∠ ABD = m ∠ BDA = (180 - 18) / 2 = 81°

In triangle CBD, two interior angles are equal to the exterior angle on the other corner. So,

m ∠ BCD + m ∠ CDB = m ∠ ABD

18 + x = 81

x = 81 - 18 = 63°

11. D
Perimeter of a triangle = sum of all three sides.
Here, Perimeter of △ABC = |AC| + |CB| + |AB|.

Since the triangle is located in the middle of two adjacent and identical rectangles, we find the side lengths using these rectangles:

|AB| = 6 + 6 = 12 cm

|CB| = 8.5 cm

|AC| = |CB| = 8.5 cm

Perimeter = |AC| + |CB| + |AB| = 8.5 + 8.5 + 12 = 29 cm

12. A
The wheel travels $2\pi r$ distance when it makes one revolution. Here, r stands for radius. The radius is given as 25 cm in the

figure. So,

$2\pi r = 2\pi * 25 = 50\pi$ cm is the distance travelled in one revolution.

In 175 revolutions: $175 * 50\pi = 8750\pi$ cm is travelled.

We are asked to find the distance in meters.

1 m = 100 cm So,

8750π cm = 8750π / 100 = 87.πm

13. B
The general formula for a hyperbola is:

$(y - k)^2 / a^2 - (x - h)^2 / b^2 = 1$ where the center is (h, k).

Now, let us convert the equation in the question into the form above to obtain the coordinates of center:

$64y^2 - 25x^2 - 384y - 100x - 1124 = 0$

$64y^2 - 384y - 25x^2 - 100x - 1124 = 0$

$64(y^2 - 6y) - 25(x^2 + 4x) - 1124 = 0$

$64(y^2 - 6y \underline{+ 9 - 9}) - 25(x^2 + 4x \underline{+ 4 - 4}) - 1124 = 0$

$64(y - 3)^2 - 64 * 9 - 25(x + 2)^2 + 25 * 4 - 1124 = 0$

$64(y - 3)^2 - 25(x + 2)^2 - 576 + 100 - 1124 = 0$

$64(y - 3)^2 - 25(x + 2)^2 = 1600$

$(64(y - 3)^2 - 25(x + 2)^2) / (64 * 25) = 1600 / (64 * 25)$

$(y - 3)^2 / 25 - (x + 2)^2 / 64 = 1$

$(y - 3)^2 / 5^2 - (x + 2)^2 / 8^2 = 1$

So, k = 3 and h = -2. The center of the hyperbola is (- 2, 3).

14. A
Equation of line d_1 is given as y = 2x + 5. The slope is equal to 2. Then, the slope of line d_2 is

2 * 2 = 4. Since lines d_2 and d_3 are perpendicular, the product of their slopes is equal to - 1:

$m_2 * m_3 = -1$

$4 * m_3 = -1$

$m_3 = -1/4$

15. B

According to Cavalieri's principle, if two solids have the same height and matching areas everywhere along the height, they have the same volume. We will calculate the volume of the pentagon prism with one side of 4 cm and height of 12 coins and this will be the result of the question.

First, let us calculate the volume of one coin. The base area of a pentagon is calculated by the formula:

A = (5/2) * s * a where s is the side length and a is the apothem. The apothem is found by:

a = s / (2tan(180/n)) where n is the number of sides. This is a pentagon, so it has 5 sides:

a = s / (2tan(180/n)) = 4 / (2tan(180/5)) = 2 / tan36 ≈ 2.75 cm

Then; A = (5/2) * s * a = (5/2) * 4 * 2.75 = 27.5 cm²

The volume of the pentagon prism is found by V = A * h. Let us find the height:

h = number of coins * height of one coin

h = 12 * 1.2 = 14.4 cm

V = 27.5 * 14.4 = 396 cm³

Part VI - Statistics and Probability

1. A
If the die is rolled for once, it can be 4, 5 or 6 since we are searching for 4 successive heads. We need to think each case separately. There are two possibilities for a coin; heads (H) or tails (T), each possibility of 1/2; we are searching for H. The possibility for a number to appear on the top of the die is 1/6. Die and coin cases are disjoint events. Also, each flip of coin is independent from the other:

Die: 4

coin: HHHH : 1 permutation

P = (1/6) * (1/2) * (1/2) * (1/2) * (1/2) = (1/6) * (1/16)

Die: 5

coin: HHHHT, THHHH, HHHHH : 3 permutations

P = (1/6) * 3 * (1/2) * (1/2) * (1/2) * (1/2) * (1/2) = (1/6) * (3/32)

Die: 6

coin: HHHHTT, TTHHHH, THHHHT, HHHHHT, THHHHH, HTHHHH, HHHHTH, HHHHHH : 8 permutations

P = (1/6) * 8 * (1/2) * (1/2) * (1/2) * (1/2) * (1/2) * (1/2) = (1/6) * (8/64)

The overall probability is:

Pall = (1/6) * (1/16) + (1/6) * (3/32) + (1/6) * (8/64)

= (1/6) * (1/16 + 3/32 + 8/64)

= (1/6) * (4 + 6 + 8) / 64 = (1/6) * (18/64) = 3/64

2. D
First add all the numbers 62 + 18 + 39 + 13 + 16 + 37 + 25 = 210. Then divide by 7 (the number of data provided) = 210/7 = 30

3. B
P(4 < X < 15) = P(X < 15) - P(X ≤ 4) = F(15) - F(4) = 1 - 0.5 = 0.5

4. B
There are 52 cards in total. If we closely observe Smith has 16 cards in which he can win. So his winning probability in a single game will be 16/52 on the other hand Simon has 20 cards of wining so his probability on win in single draw is 20/52.

5. B
80 out of 120 expect to eat out 5 days next month. This information gives the proportion of people expecting to eat out to total number of people. However, not all employees participated the survey; so we accept that the random sample represents all employees:

If 80 out of 120 expect to eat out next month, how many employees out of 450 expect to eat out?

450 * 80 / 120 = 300 employees

6. D
The most frequent occurring number in the series (90, 80, 77, 86, 90, 91, 77, 66, 69, 65, 43, 65, 75, 43, 90) is 90

7. B
At first glance; we can think that a child can be either a girl or a boy, so the probability for the other child to be a girl is 1/2. However, we need to think deeper. The combinations of two children can be as follows:

boy + girl

boy + boy

girl + boy

girl + girl

So, the sample space is S = {BG, BB, GB, GG} where the sequence is important.

Sarah has a girl; this is the fact. So, calling this as event A, here are the possibilities:

boy + girl

girl + boy

girl + girl

We eliminate boy + boy, since one child is a girl. A = {BG, GB, GG}

The event that Sarah has two girls: B = {GG}

We need to compute:

P(B|A. = P(B ∩ A. / P(A. = 1/3

8. B
Notice that 3 out of 9 damaged bulbs should be chosen to have exactly 3 damaged bulbs. Since 3 bulbs are chosen, we have (12 - 3 = 9) 9 bulbs to choose further, within the safe bulbs. These 9 bulbs should be chosen from 100 - 9 damaged = 93 safe bulbs. These two cases are multiplied as follows:

C(9, 3) * C(93, 9)

The total number of possible ways of choosing 12 bulbs out of 100 is found by:

C(100, 12)

The probability is:

(C(9, 3) * C(93, 9)) / C(100, 12)

= ((9! / (6! * 3!)) * (93! / (84! * 9!))) / (100! / (88! * 12!))

= ((9 * 8 * 7 * 6!) / (6! * 3!)) * ((93 * 92 * 91 . ... . 84!) / (84! * 9!)) * ((88! * 12!) / (100 * 99 * 98 . ... . 88!))

= 84 * ((12 * 11 * 10 * 9!) / 9!) * ((93 * 92 * 91 . ... . 85) / (100 * 99 * 98 . ... . 89))

= (84 * 12 * 11 * 10) * (88 * 87 * 86 * 85) / (100 * 99 * 98 * 97 * 96 * 95 * 94) = (11 * 29 * 43 * 17) / (5 * 7 * 97 * 47 * 19)

= 0.076916... ≈ 0.08

9. A

Let the number of red balls be x

Then number of blue balls = 2x - 5

Then number of green balls = 2(2x - 5) + 3 = 4x - 10 + 3

= 4x - 7

As there are total 30 balls so the equation becomes

x + 2x - 5 + 4x - 7 = 30

x = 6

Red balls are 6, blue are 7 and green are 17.
As the probability of drawing a red ball is twice than the others, let's take them as 12. So the total number of balls will be 36.

Probability of drawing the 1st red: 12/36
Probability of drawing the 2nd red: 10/34

Combined probability = 12/36 X 10/34 = 10/102

10. D

First, let us find the all possible results for X + Y depending on the number seen on the die. The set of the numbers on the die is as follows:

S = {1, 2, 3, 4, 5, 6}

(X + Y)(S) = X(S) + Y(S) because these are disjoint events. Remember that X(S) is two times the number and Y is 1 if the number is odd and 3 if the number is even.

Then;

(X + Y)(1) = X(1) + Y(1) = 2 + 1 = 3

(X + Y)(2) = X(2) + Y(2) = 4 + 3 = 7

$(X + Y)(3) = X(3) + Y(3) = 6 + 1 = 7$

$(X + Y)(4) = X(4) + Y(4) = 8 + 3 = 11$

$(X + Y)(5) = X(5) + Y(5) = 10 + 1 = 11$

$(X + Y)(6) = X(6) + Y(6) = 12 + 3 = 15$

So, $(X + Y)(S) = \{3, 7, 11, 15\}$

Now, let us draw the results - probabilities table:

z_i	3	7	11	15
$P(z_i)$	1/6	2/6	2/6	1/6

$E(X + Y)$
$= \sum_{i=1}^{m} z_i * P(z_i)$

$= 3 * (1/6) + 7 * (2/6) + 11 * (2/6) + 15 *(1/6)$
$= 54/6 = 9$

Conclusion

CONGRATULATIONS! You have made it this far because you have applied yourself diligently to practicing for the exam and no doubt improved your potential score considerably! Getting into a good school is a huge step in a journey that might be challenging at times but will be many times more rewarding and fulfilling. That is why being prepared is so important.

Good Luck!

FREE Ebook Version

Download a FREE Ebook version of the publication!

Suitable for tablets, iPad, iPhone, or any smart phone.

Go to http://tinyurl.com/hxdvdwb

www.ingramcontent.com/pod-product-compliance
Lightning Source LLC
Chambersburg PA
CBHW070900080526
44589CB00013B/1142